Kitty Muggeridge

GAZING
ON TRUTH

Meditations on Reality

GRAND RAPIDS, MICHIGAN
WILLIAM B. EERDMANS PUBLISHING COMPANY

ACKNOWLEDGMENTS
Biblical quotations are from the Authorized Version of the Bible,
which is Crown Copyright, and are used by permission.

Extracts from the Book of Common Prayer of 1662,
which is Crown Copyright,
are reproduced by permission of Eyre & Spottiswoode,
Her Majesty's Printers, London.

Extracts from 'The Glory of the Garden' © 1911 and
'When Earth's Last Picture' © 1892 by Rudyard Kipling
are used by permission of the National Trust.

Library of Congress Cataloging in Publication Data
Muggeridge, Kitty.
Gazing on truth.

1. Devotional calendars.   2. Lent — Prayer-books and
devotions — English.   I. Title.
BV4812.M84   1985   242   85-4393

ISBN 0-8028-0072-6 (pbk.)

For Malcolm, who helped

Contents

20 February 1956

*The first Sunday in Lent repeatedly returns to us
the tragic scene of the Great Temptations of the Son
of Man. To this day it is repeated in the history of
man, in the life of Christ's Church, in the soul of
every Christian. It is a blessing that Christ let it be
shown on Him what methods the tempter uses,
what his seductive traps consist of. Do I not observe
in myself how susceptible I am to the temptation of
'bread', to the temptation of an easy life, to the
temptation of being left in peace? . . . Today many
people . . . allow themselves to be borne on the
arms of evil spirits because they constantly fall flat
on their faces, paying servile homage to all
tempters . . . Am I to be scandalized by them? No,
rather I should grow wiser, so that I myself will not
be tempted by the devil.'*

From *A Freedom from Within*, the prison notes of
Stefan, Cardinal Wyszynski

1 *What is Real?*

In a materialistic age like ours nothing is real except what is false.

   M.

~~~~~~

These meditations aim to help strengthen our faith and to defy the 'dictatorship of the consensus'; to help us forget our preoccupation with the fantasies of our earthly existence, and to discover and be aware of spiritual reality, which alone reveals what is true, and brings us closer to God.

Our attention is constantly being drawn in these days to a kaleidoscope of news and gossip which imprisons us in the dark fantasy of unreality, so that we cannot perceive the truth of spiritual reality. For what we see with our eyes and hear with our ears, we are inclined to believe, and as the poet Blake warns us, we are led to believe a lie 'when you see *with*, not thro', the Eye'.

Thomas à Kempis exhorts us to avoid public gatherings as much as possible, for 'discussion of worldly affairs becomes a great hindrance to discovering what is real even though it be with the best intentions, for we are quickly corrupted and ensnared by vanity.' If we resolve to avoid unnecessary talk and listening to news and gossip, we shall have plenty of time to spend in meditation on what is holy.

Genetics, technology, science and political theories – these are the fake mysticism of our era. They persuade us to believe in a utopian age to come, in which pain, suffering, evil and death will be eliminated, putting us, as it were, on Caliban's Island which

> . . . is full of noises,
> Sounds, and sweet airs, that give delight and hurt not:
> Sometimes a thousand twanging instruments
> Will hum about mine ears; and sometimes voices,
> That, if I then had waked after long sleep,
> Will make me sleep again – and then, in dreaming,
> The clouds methought would open, and show riches
> Ready to drop upon me, that when I waked
> I cried to dream again.
>
>   The Tempest

1

The late Professor Jacques Monod, the famous French geneticist and Nobel prize winner, in the course of a television session in Toronto with Mother Teresa, spoke of how in his opinion all our destiny was locked up in our genes, which shape and direct our character and outlook, thus destroying the individual. As he held forth on this theme, Mother Teresa sat with her eyes closed and her hands folded, deep in prayer. On being asked by the programme's compère whether she had anything to say, she replied: 'I believe in love and compassion,' and resumed her devotions.

As the Professor was leaving the studio he was heard to mutter: 'If I saw much more of that woman I should be in bad trouble!'

Mother Teresa answers our dilemma as to what is real and what is false; truth, she tells us, can only be grasped by faith in God's love for us, as it exists in the depths of each individual soul.

2 Why Fast?

Take no thought for your life, what ye shall eat, or what ye shall drink; nor yet for your body, what ye shall put on.

Matthew 6.25

~~~~~~

Fasting has been practised throughout the ages by believers of all religions. It is designed to strengthen our spiritual life by rejecting the enticements of the pleasures of the senses. This Lent fast of forty days is recommended by Jesus by example and teaching. These lines by Robert Herrick tell us how to keep a true Lent:

> Is it to quit the dish
>   Of Flesh, yet still
>   To fill
> The platter high with Fish?
>
> To shew a heart grief-rent;
>   To starve thy sin,
>   Not Bin;
> And that's to keep thy Lent.

From 'To keep a True Lent'

Following in the steps of Jesus means daily dying to self. Yet Jesus himself turned the water into wine at the wedding feast in Cana. In our human circumstances, while feeding the soul we must humbly admit that we need also to feed the body, gratefully accepting what God provides, whether it be much or little. In our daily lives we need to starve our inclination to self-indulgence and vanity. Lovers of this world, Thomas à Kempis reminds us, are often misled by their exclusive passion for visible things. While you live in the flesh the burden of the flesh will prove a sorrow to you, for it will not let you devote yourself to the contemplation of God.

Advertising is the great purveyor of these enticing fantasies. It is a contemporary tower of Babel (which Milton called 'The high Tower of Satan's Kingdom') broadcasting Satan's message urging us to eat more, dress more, spend more, smoke more. As the motorist approaches the little towns along the American highways neon signs spell out the good news from heaven below – FOOD,

3

BEAUTY, DRUGS, GAS – four pillars of what Bunyan calls Vanity Fair and we call the Affluent Society.

The first time Mother Teresa was in a New York television studio, a touch of whimsicality was provided by Providence.

That particular morning the commercials were all about different varieties of packaged bread and other foods, commended to viewers as being non-fattening and non-nourishing. It took some time for the irony to strike home, Mother Teresa's own constant preoccupation being, of course, to find the wherewithal to nourish the starving and put some flesh on human skeletons. When it did, she was heard to remark in a quiet but perfectly audible voice: 'I see that Christ is needed in television studios.' . . . a word of truth had been spoken in one of the mills of fantasy where the great twentieth century myth of happiness successfully pursued is fabricated. A sudden silence descended on the studio . . .

A Gift for God

~~~~~~

Let Milton have the last word:

> *What in me is dark*
> *Illumine, what is low raise and support;*
> *That to the highth of this great Argument*
> *I may assert Eternal Providence,*
> *And justify the ways of God to men.*

From 'Paradise Lost'

4

3　The Mystery of Faith

*Faith is the substance of things hoped for, the evidence of things
not seen. . . . Through faith we understand that the worlds were
framed by the word of God, so that things which are seen were
not made of things which do appear.*

Hebrews 11.1, 3

The entire story of man on earth has no meaning at all except a
religious meaning. 'There is no hope except in a vast increase of
spiritual religion' (Arnold Toynbee).

Today in the West, the claims of science and the theory of
evolution are persuading many of us to believe in things seen, and
to hope for things of this world. G. K. Chesterton remarked that
when men no longer believe in God they don't believe in nothing;
this would be bad enough; but they believe in anything.

Progress in technology and the development of industry brings
us ever-increasing affluence. The prospect of this ever-increasing
gross national product makes us proud and arrogant. We believe
that we can, by ourselves, create a heaven on earth; a Utopia in
which everyone will enjoy health, wealth and happiness and lead
a peaceful, self-fulfilled life. All will be right with the world. We
discover, on the contrary, that ever-increasing affluence brings
ever-increasing greed, envy, hatred, strife, madness and despair.
Our utopian heaven on earth is an empty dream. We have reached
a dead end. 'Why am I here? What am I? What is the meaning of
life?' we ask.

Belief in wealth has been the ruin of many great nations. When
St Augustine heard that Rome had been sacked he remarked: 'Men
build cities and men destroy them,' and added, 'but the city of God
men did not build and cannot destroy.'

There is a fairy story about a wealthy merchant, loaded with riches,
who was in despair. He wondered why. He asked his companions
how he could find happiness. 'Look for a happy man,' they told him,
'and ask him to give you his shirt.' The merchant searched for a long
time until at last he found a happy man. 'Give me your shirt,' he said.
'I can pay for it.' The happy man began to laugh uproariously; he
hadn't got a shirt! Then the merchant understood the cause of his
own despair: man cannot live by bread alone.

5

We long to believe in some spiritual dimension outside ourselves. We are like the father who brought his son to Jesus to be cured of his madness. Jesus told him: 'All things are possible to him that believeth.' Then the father wept and cried out: 'Lord, I believe; help thou mine unbelief.'

It is when we look beyond time that we catch a glimpse of eternity and begin to accept the mystery of things, to be aware of our unknowable Creator, of God who loves us. No one can fail to notice the glorious beauty of creation all about us. The rising and setting of the sun; moonlit nights; the scent of flowers; the song of birds, music and human love and human joy, all proclaim that city of God which man cannot destroy. Then our faith is renewed. It is like a message sent to help our unbelief. If we listen, we shall be able to say with conviction in our heart: 'I believe in God the father, Maker of heaven and earth. . . .'

———————————————————————————————

To see a world in a grain of sand
And a heaven in a wild flower,
Hold infinity in the palm of your hand
And Eternity in an hour.

He who replies to words of doubt,
Doth put the light of knowledge out.
A riddle, or the cricket's cry
Is to doubt a fit reply.

He who doubts from what he sees
Will ne'er believe, do what you please.
If the sun and moon should doubt,
They'd immediately go out.

William Blake, from
'Auguries of Innocence'

4 Freedom

Stand fast therefore in the liberty wherewith Christ hath made us free, and be not entangled again with the yoke of bondage.

Galatians 5.1.

Men have always pursued freedom. In the name of freedom wars have been fought, revolutions have broken out, Utopias have been dreamt of, cults have been practised and ideological states have been set up. The Communist Manifesto declared that man, born free, is everywhere in chains, and prescribed a remedy for this unsatisfactory state of affairs, out of which emerged, not the glorious freedom envisaged, but the most brutal dictatorship that has ever enslaved man.

Now the quest for freedom is becoming personal rather than political. It is a quest for self-hood, and its outcome is no better. When self-denial goes out of fashion, self-fulfilment takes its place. In their pursuit of self-fulfilment, liberated women are prepared to sacrifice their families. With their battle-cry of 'Women must decide their fate, not the Church and not the State', they are willing to allow the State to decide the fate of their children, if they have any. The cry raised after the French revolution, 'O Liberty, O Liberty, what crimes have been committed in thy name!' might well be applied to the crime of abortion. The murder of unborn children has become a holocaust.

Self-fulfilment soon grows into a quest for self-indulgence with a vocabulary of I, Me, Mine and self-indulgence, in turn, soon becomes unbridled. The self-indulgent pursuit of pleasure embraces tolerance of homosexuality, addiction to eroticism, addiction to drugs and alcohol, habitual divorce, vandalism and lawlessness. Thus liberty becomes libertinism. It is a dictatorship of permissiveness which enslaves its citizens, a dictatorship whose decrees are endlessly purveyed by the media.

The part played by the media was demonstrated not long ago during an outbreak of violence in Detroit which the police were unable to control. It was only when they ordered that such acts should not be shown to the public on television screens that the rioting ceased and law and order were restored. In the name, not

7

of freedom but of money, cable television conveys to the public acts of eroticism which compete with any brothel.

Alexander Solzhenitsyn recalls how he first encountered freedom when he was a prisoner in a labour camp of the Gulag Archipelago in Soviet Russia. He noticed that a fellow prisoner in the bunk above him seemed always to be serene and happy. This prisoner suffered the cruelty of his gaolers without resentment. He patiently endured the hardships inflicted on him in that horrible place. He cheerfully submitted to insults and obediently carried out the arduous task allotted to him. When the day was over, he climbed up to his bunk and spent the evening happily absorbed in reading from a bundle of loose sheets of paper covered in handwriting. Solzhenitsyn asked him what kept him so contented and cheerful. He replied that it was God's Word, revealed to him in the Bible copied out by hand on those loose sheets of paper.

This is where we can find true freedom: the freedom which will release us from bondage to the fantasy of self-fulfilment and libertinism; the freedom which will open our eyes to 'the glorious liberty of the children of God; the freedom to choose good and reject evil.

'O God, who art the author of peace and lover of concord, in knowledge of whom standeth our eternal life, whose service is perfect freedom: Defend us thy humble servants in all assaults of our enemies.

. . . Give unto thy servants that peace which the world cannot give.

Book of Common Prayer

5 Peace

*In the world ye shall have tribulation: but be of good cheer; I
have overcome the world.*

John 16.33.

The devastating prospect of nuclear warfare has called into being
a number of militant pacifist movements urging disarmament. But
they shout their slogans to little effect. It was the same after the
first and second world wars. The League of Nations, The Women's
International League for Peace and Freedom, and many disarmament conferences flooded into Geneva all in the cause of pacifism.

Senor Maderiaga, the Spanish delegate to one of these intermin-
able disarmament conferences, told a fable which demonstrates the
inevitable outcome of their demands: the animals in the jungle got
together with a view to living at peace with one another. The tiger
eloquently proposed that the eagle should have his talons removed;
the elephant suggested that the wolf should have his fangs removed;
the hedgehog that the adder should sick up all his poison; until at
last the Russian bear opened his arms and invited all present to
join him in a loving hug.

Most of us hate war and love peace, but if the demands of the
various movements for disarmament were met we might well find
ourselves in the same predicament. Like the animals in that fable,
if we are defenceless we must be prepared to submit to the embrace
of any predatory invader seeking power by brute force. As the
Pope has recently pointed out, weapons, whether they are nuclear
missiles or crossbows, do not themselves cause wars. Wars are
waged by the men who use them.

'I am ashamed,' said Katharina in *The Taming of the Shrew*, 'that
women are so simple to offer war where they should kneel for
peace.' Pacifism is a general idea. Peace is a spiritual truth. And
they will always be estranged.

Mother Teresa has never in her life joined a peace movement or
taken part in a peace march. When her name was being considered
for the Nobel Peace Prize award, the query was: 'What has this
woman done for peace?' The judges were not able to resist the
reply that Mother Teresa draws her strength from her divine
Master by dedicating her life to love and compassion. She is an

9

instrument of his peace. She and her sisters of charity are the messengers who spread the gospel of peace in the world. If she had a slogan it would be 'Kneeling for Peace'. Her favourite prayer, attributed to St Francis, is:

Lord make me an instrument of Thy peace. Where there is hatred, let me sow love; where there is injury, pardon; where there is doubt, faith; where there is despair, hope; where there is sadness, joy; where there is darkness, light.

If we are looking for lasting peace we shall find it in that peace that passes understanding which Jesus alone can give us.

My soul, there is a country
Far beyond the stars,
Where stands a winged sentry
All skilful in the wars:
There above noise and danger
Sweet Peace sits crowned with smiles,
And One born in a manger
Commands the beauteous files.

If thou canst get but thither,
There grows the flower of Peace,
The Rose that cannot wither,
Thy fortress, and thy ease.

Henry Vaughan, from 'Peace'

6   Heavens Below

My kingdom is not of this world.
John 18.36

Behold, the kingdom of God is within you.
Luke 14.20

Since Jesus lived, men have longed for a Kingdom of Heaven on earth, a Kingdom in which men and women live together harmoniously, in peace, prosperity and perfect happiness. Sir Thomas More described such a kingdom in a book he called *Utopia*, a word derived from the Greek meaning No Land. It was, he wrote, 'A fruitful and pleasunt worke of the beste State of a public weale, and of the new yle Utopia.' Later *News from Nowhere* by William Morris, and *Erehwon* ('nowhere' spelt backwards) by Samuel Butler were books about the same subject.

In the late nineteenth and early twentieth centuries many Utopias were founded on the philosophies of men like William Morris and Ruskin. To them the Kingdom of Heaven was a collective conception where all goodness was social goodness. 'The work of each for weal of all' was their creed and a bee replaced the cross of Christianity. Their ethics were: a simple life, public ownership and free love. They lived on what they could produce by digging the earth. In one Utopia, inspired by the writings of Tolstoy, the members enthusiastically tore up the title deeds of the land they had bought and destroyed their marriage lines. The result was that their more worldly neighbours encroached little by little on their property, and trouble and strife arose between husband and wife. These social Utopias were attempts at providing a way of living a godly righteous and sober life without the cross of Christianity. Not many of them have survived.

The Communist Utopia in Russia, the Welfare Utopia in England and the Affluent Utopia in America all began with the same trust in social goodness. Today all three are in a state of disarray and near collapse. A fourth has appeared on the horizon, the Mechanical Utopia. But this too is beginning to disappoint our hopes. The mechanical heaven of Disney's Wonderland is rapidly being replaced by the mechanical hell of nuclear missiles, acid rain

11

and 'video nasties'. In the eighteenth century Pascal wrote this warning:

> It is in vain for men to look for a cure for all their miseries. Philosophers have promised them to you, but have not been able to keep their promise . . . your principal maladies are pride, which cuts you off from God; sensuality, which binds you to the earth. If they have given you God for your object it has only been to pander to your pride.

'No-Landers' are looking collectively for a Kingdom of Heaven through the dark windows of their mortality. But the Kingdom of Heaven is a country which can only be seen by the light of the spirit which shines in each soul. If we set out for it alone we shall reach it together.

> *Not in Utopia, – subterranean fields, –*
> *Or some secreted island, Heaven knows where!*
> *But in the very world, which is the world*
> *Of all of us, – the place where, in the end,*
> *We find our happiness, or not at all!*
>
> William Wordsworth, from 'The Prelude'

7 God's Messenger

How beautiful upon the mountains are the feet of him that
bringeth good tidings, that publisheth peace; that bringeth good
tidings of good, that publisheth salvation.

Isaiah 52.7

'In all history,' wrote Simone Weil in *Waiting on God*, 'souls have
never been in such peril as they are today in every part of the
globe.' But God in his mercy, has sent a messenger, as he always
has done in such times of crisis, to demonstrate his gospel of love.
It is Mother Teresa of Calcutta whom he has sent to guide souls out
of the dark abyss that prevails in the world today.

Mother Teresa has dedicated her life to God. She and her sisters
undertake to observe four vows: to follow Christ with undivided
love in chastity and in total obedience; to love unconditionally
without seeking returns or results; to love in chastity in a spirit of
total surrender; to love in poverty.

Politics to Mother Teresa are an irrelevance. 'There are those,'
she says, 'who struggle for justice in the world and for human
rights and try to change structures.' Her mission is to look at the
problems individually. 'If a person feels that God wants him to
pledge for the collective change of social structures, this is a
question between God and himself.' For her revolution comes from
God and is made of love. Mother Teresa never judges others. The
harshest comment she ever makes, even about the most villainous,
is that she has met 'Jesus in a very distressing disguise'. This
attitude has enabled her to open houses in countries under
communist rule, among the victims of want and despair and
oppression in East Germany and Yugoslavia. When she applied for
permission for her sisters to work among the starving people of
Ethiopia the following dialogue took place:

'What do you want from the Government?'

'Nothing. I have only come to offer my sisters to work among
the poorest suffering people.'

'What will your sisters do?'

'We give wholehearted service to the poorest of the poor.'

'What qualifications do you have?'

13

'We try to bring tender love and compassion to the unwanted and unloved.'

'I see you have quite a different approach. Do you preach to the people, trying to convert them?'

'Our work of love reveals to the suffering poor the love of God for them.'

This interview received the following response from the eighty year old Emperor Haile Salassie: 'I have heard about the good works you do. I am very happy you have come. Yes, let your sisters come to Ethiopia.'

This illustrates the way Mother Teresa confronts the wisdom of man with the love of God. And the love of God always prevails.

She is remembered by those who were her fellow novices as having been remarkable for her ordinariness. In her actions and in her words and in her whole being she contradicts every view cherished and propagated by the media and the consensus of opinion today. And yet her name is known and venerated throughout the world. She and her Sisters of Charity set out 'to quench the thirst of Jesus Christ on the Cross'.

'There is nothing among human beings that has such power to keep our gaze fixed ever more intensely upon God, than the friendship of the friends of God,' wrote Simone Weil. Mother Teresa, God's friend, is keeping the eyes of all her friends fixed on God. She is the kindly light who will lead us to his kingdom. She has about her the beauty of holiness. She also has the beauty of shrewdness. These are gifts from God whereby she can show souls how to be in the world but not of it. She is the light that leads souls to where they can recognize Jesus in every disguise. Let Mother Teresa be our friend.

Lead, kindly Light, amid the encircling gloom,
Lead thou me on;
The night is dark, and I am far from home,
Lead thou me on.
Keep thou my feet; I do not ask to see
The distant scene; one step enough for me.

Cardinal Newman

8 *The Sacrament of the Present Moment*

Trust the past to God's mercy, the present to His love, and the future to His providence.

St Augustine

We spend a great deal of time during our life on earth looking into the future or back into the past. We worry about a nuclear holocaust; we worry about our future finances; we anxiously await the result of some enterprise. We plan for a future that may never happen.

If we are not looking into the future we look back on the past. We recall past happiness. We regret missed opportunities. We wish we hadn't done those things we ought not to have done. All this is of no avail. The future is unknown and the past is irretrievable. The fourteenth century author of the *Cloud of Unknowing* told his disciple to 'Let the backwards be'. He added, 'Look now forward'. Doubtless he was thinking of eternity.

In Tolstoy's story, *How much Land does a Man require?* Pakhom, a peasant, spends much time planning to become a rich landowner. He goes with his savings to a man who has land and enquires the price. 'As much land as you can walk round in a day', is the answer. So Pakhom puts all his money in his cap on the ground to mark the place from where he is to start. At sunrise he sets off briskly. At midday it begins to grow hot. Determined not to stop for rest, he thinks only of the acres that are going to be his. As evening draws on he is tired and hungry. He walks on, determined to take in a bit more land. Finally, as the sun sinks behind the horizon, he reaches the spot from where he started. As he reaches out for his money he falls dead. He spent each moment of that day planning his future but at the end of it, he is dead. His dream of owning land is buried with him. They both soak away out of time into the past.

Our conscious existence on earth is reduced to the present moment. It is in the present moment, continually dripping into time from the future and soaking away into the past, that we live and have our being. And it is in this dimension that we take decisions to fulfil whatever tasks our circumstances or duty require, or make impulsive decisions which have no connection with our will or reason. Most of us have experienced a sudden urge to visit a friend whom we have not seen or thought of for a long time, only to discover that he is in dire need of our help. These mysterious impulses, which always have good intention, are inspired by our heart and come from the spirit within us. When we obey them we find they are a direct communication from God.

'. . . such acts have essentially all the merit and value good intentions always have. . . . God's purpose, the being and essence of God, becomes the object of these intentions and God unites himself to them without stint or measure. And if that eternal love partly ends in the senses it is because God's will does too . . . God can communicate with the heart because, having been emptied of everything by the infinite power of his perfect love, the heart is pure and undefiled and so redeemed and made fit to receive him.'

De Caussade, *The Sacrament of the Present Moment*

A thousand ages in thy sight
Are like an evening gone,
Short as the watch that ends the night
Before the rising sun.

Time, like an ever-rolling stream,
Bears all its sons away;
They fly forgotten, as a dream
Dies at the opening day.

Isaac Watts

9   *Now and Always*

*Take therefore no thought for the morrow: for the morrow shall
take thought for the things of itself. Sufficient unto the day is the
evil thereof.*

Matthew 6.34

Now is Always and Always is Now. Time and eternity, like body
and soul, cannot be separated. This is a revelation, as it were, of
the incarnation, of God in eternity becoming Man in time. It is the
foundation of the Christian faith.

If we consider Now separately from Always, we tend to look on
the past with regret and to the future with hope or foreboding. But
the past no longer exists and tomorrow never comes. Only Now
exists Always.

If we take Now more seriously than Always, time more seriously
than eternity, we become concerned with the material quality of
life. We set up utopian organizations to relieve injustice, hunger
and suffering. But governments and politics do not enrich the
quality of life, or remove the causes of injustice and strife.

If we take Always more seriously than Now, eternity more
seriously than time, we are in danger of 'advocating a lofty scorn
of this maimed and suffering world while we bask on the sunny
shores of the eternal'. Now and Always must never be separated.

'Now is Always and Always is Now' is described by the Jesuit
Jean Pierre de Caussade as 'the Sacrament of the Present Moment'.

It is in the present moment that God reveals to us his purpose.
It is He who decides what we shall do and when, and not
ourselves. It is His will that directs us and must replace all other
guidance. Reduced to the dimensions of the present moment it
can reach our senses and pass into our heart. We must unre-
servedly surrender ourselves to His will for it is God alone that
quickens the soul in the creature and the creature in the soul.

We must look on the present moment as though nothing else in
the world matters. Every condition of body and soul, everything
that happens in time, inwardly or outwardly, what each moment
reveals, is God's divine purpose. This is the Sacrament of the
Present Moment; even when everything else seems to be telling us

17

something different, we must abandon ourselves to His divine providence saying, 'Thy will, not mine, be done now and always.'

~~~~~~

Jesus, by his Godhead, is maker and giver of time. He by his manhood is the truest heeder of time and He by his Godhead and Manhood is the truest judge and asker of account of the spending of time.

The Cloud of Unknowing

10 The Beauty of the Earth

God said: 'And to every beast of the earth, and to every fowl of the air, and to every thing that creepeth upon the earth, wherein there is life, I have given every green herb for meat: and it was so. And God saw everything that he had made, and, behold, it was very good.'

Genesis 1.30, 31

~~~~~~

A patient in a psychiatric hospital said to his visitor: 'You know, when I look out of the window at all the clouds, and the trees, and the birds; the moon and the stars and the sun, I see God in them all.'

Everyone in the room looked up astonished and interested.

'Do you? So do I. Isn't that wonderful!' answered the visitor.

The patient looked puzzled and said: 'But it was because I talked in this way that they put me here.'

William Blake, who was also considered mad, saw nature with the same mystical eye:

> The sun descending in the west,
> The evening star does shine;
> The birds are silent in their nest,
> And I must seek for mine,
> The moon like a flower,
> In Heaven's high bower;
> With silent delight,
> Sits and smiles on the night.
>
> Farewell green leaves and happy groves,
> Where flocks have took delight;
> Where lambs have nibbled; silent moves
> The feet of angels bright;
> Unseen they pour blessing,
> And joy without ceasing,
> On each bud and blossom,
> And each sleeping bosom.
>
> From 'Night'

The insane are often more in touch with spiritual truth than the

19

sane. Perhaps this is why in the East they are revered and not drugged.

There is more evidence for the creation of the earth than for the theory of evolution. We call our Creator, God, and his divine beauty is reflected on earth. Each year the seasons reflect the stages in our journey through life. Spring is our youth; summer our manhood; autumn our old age and winter our death. Death is followed by darkness, the silvery moon and spring again, which is eternity. Thus God speaks to us in parables.

Nature is all around us. The green leaves of spring, the scent of flowers, the song of birds, and butterflies in summer; the golden autumn with ripening fruit, and tiny creeping things, the bare branches of winter, all declare the beauty of God's creation. Even in the polluted air of great cities there flourish green parks and little flower-filled gardens to distract us from the noisy traffic, crowded streets and fashionable shops. As we look at them we are reminded of Jesus who told his followers to consider the lilies. They toil not, neither do they spin, yet even Solomon in all his glory was not arrayed like one of them.

Musicians, artists and poets all celebrate the beauty of the earth. William Wordsworth sings its praises in his 'Ode on the Intimations of Immortality':

> The Rainbow comes and goes,
> And lovely is the Rose,
> The Moon doth with delight
> Look round her when the heavens are bare,
> Waters on a starry night
> Are beautiful and fair;
> The sunshine is a glorious birth;
>
> Now, while the birds thus sing their joyous song,
> And while the young lambs bound
> As to the tabor's sound . . .
> I hear the Echoes through the mountains, throng,
> The Winds come to me from the fields of sleep,
> And all the earth is gay;
> Land and sea,
> Give themselves up to jollity,
> And with the heart of May
> Doth every Beast keep holiday.

20

When we contemplate nature we are called away from worldly distractions, from what Blaise Pascal called licking the earth. We rejoice and are filled with hope. The beauty all around us revives our spirit. It is the spring of living water from which we drink to refresh our thirsty souls. The beauty of the earth is a testimony of the Holy Spirit. It is a precious legacy which we cannot ignore.

For the beauty of the earth,
For the beauty of the skies,
For the love which from our birth
Over and around us lies,
Lord of all, to thee we raise,
This our grateful hymn of praise.

For the beauty of each hour,
Of the day and of the night.
Hill and vale, and tree and flower,
Sun and moon and stars of light,
Lord of all, to thee we raise,
This our grateful hymn of praise.

F. S. Pierpoint

11 *Gardening*

*And the Lord shall guide thee continually, and satisfy thy soul
in drought, and make fat thy bones, and thou shalt be like a
watered garden, and like a spring of water, whose waters fail
not.*

Isaiah 58.11

Everyone loves gardens. Green parks with their bright flowers
gladden the eyes of city dwellers. Visitors delight in the lovely
grounds surrounding stately homes when they are thrown open to
the public. The little cultivated patches round each humble
dwelling bring joy and satisfaction to their owners. Even those who
live in high rise buildings on deserts of concrete love to cultivate
window boxes and water the potted plants in their sitting rooms.
And who does not love to plant a garden of flowers over the grave
of a loved one?

Almighty God himself made the first garden. Adam was his
gardener. When Mary Magdalene saw Jesus in the Garden she
took him for the gardener.

But as Rudyard Kipling wrote:

gardens . . . are not made
by singing: 'Oh, how beautiful!' and sitting in the shade. . . .

Oh, Adam was a gardener, and God who made him sees
That half a proper gardener's work is done upon his knees,
So when your work is finished you can wash your hands and
   pray
For the Glory of the Garden, that it may not pass away!
And the Glory of the Garden it shall never pass away!

From 'The Glory of the Garden'

Like Adam, gardeners must dig the earth, uproot the weeds and
fight the pests which attack our plants. Then we shall see these
plants reaching up towards the light while their roots push down
into the dark earth.

Gardening keeps us in touch with reality more than any other
activity. It can teach us to be gardeners of our souls, for, like the
plants we cultivate, our bodies are rooted in the darkness of

22

mortality while our souls look up to the light of heaven. We learn to root out our sins which threaten to destroy us as the weeds in our garden threaten to destroy our plants. We fight temptations as we do the garden pests. If we are gardeners of our souls God will quench our thirst with living water just as he sends his rain down upon our gardens when the earth is dry and parched.

~~~~~~

> *A garden is a lovesome thing, God wot!*
> *Rose plot,*
> *Fringed pool,*
> *Fern'd grot,*
> *The veriest school*
> *Of peace; and yet the fool*
> *Contends that God is not –*
> *Not God! in gardens! when the eve is cool?*
> *Nay, but I have a sign;*
> *'Tis very sure God walks in mine.*

Thomas Edward Brown, from 'My Garden'

12   *Waiting on God*

Rest in the Lord, and wait patiently for him. . . .
Wait on the Lord, and keep his way. . . .

Psalm 37.7, 34

Simone Weil in her book *Waiting on God* wrote that nothing among human beings has such power to keep our gaze fixed ever more intensely upon God, than friendship for the friends of God.

Waiting on God calls for a perfect confidence in God alone. It means despising the appeal of what appears powerful and illustrious in the world and surrendering ourselves to his providence, saying: 'Thy will, not mine, be done. . . .' This is not the exclusive practice of any particular theology, creed or group of believers. It is the heart of religion itself.

Waiting on God also involves our relation with time, and entails devoting ourselves to his service in our daily actions as well as in our hearts. In the words of John Woolman, the Quaker, it 'keeps us close to that which is pure within us and which leads us up to Him'.

Deep in us all, Christians and non-Christians alike, there is a longing to commune with God. Tolstoy tells the story of Martin, the old shoemaker, who longed to die. A pilgrim told him that it was because he lived entirely for his own pleasure.

'For what should I live?' asked Martin.

'For God alone,' was the reply.

'How?' asked Martin.

'Read the Old Testament,' replied the pilgrim.

So Martin read, and as he read he grew happier and happier. He began to live for God alone. One night he heard a voice in his sleep calling him: 'Martin, look into the street tomorrow. I am coming to visit you.' Martin rose early and watched expectantly at the window. Presently an old soldier, bent and cold, knocked at his door. Martin invited him in and gave him some hot soup. Then a woman with her baby shivering with cold knocked. He took them in and fed and clothed them. Again there was a third knock and an old apple woman stood at the door, and Martin gave her shelter. Martin waited on, but no one else came.

That night as he was falling asleep a voice whispered in his ear: 'Martin, dost thou not know me?'

'Who art thou?' asked Martin.

'Even I.'

The old soldier appeared, whispered, 'Lo, it is I!' and vanished.

'It is I!' whispered a second voice, and the woman with her baby appeared and vanished.

'It is I!' whispered a third voice and the old apple woman appeared and was gone.

Then Martin realized that Jesus had visited him that day and he had received him. He had waited on God and God had come to him.

So let us, with patience and true humility, wait on God whose presence, when it comes, shines his divine light on the dark fantasy of our earthly life, and let us 'entrust the past to God's mercy, the present to his love, and the future to his providence' (St Augustine).

God be in my head and in my understanding;
God be in my eyes, and in my looking;
God be in my mouth, and in my speaking;
God be in my heart, and in my thinking;
God be at my end, and at my departing.

Anon c. 1514

13   *Humility*

Blessed are the meek: for they shall inherit the earth.

Matthew 5.5

Better it is to be of an humble spirit with the lowly, than to divide the spoil with the proud.

Proverbs 16.19

Humility is not a greatly esteemed virtue today. According to the teaching of some contemporary psychologists, we should pursue our ambition, rely on our talents, and satisfy rather than suppress our desires and appetites. We shall then become successful, self-fulfilled citizens in our materialistic society.

Nevertheless, humility is the source of our spiritual life. Despising our human arrogance we must subject our reason to God's will. This calls for total submission to him – although we must be careful not to fall into the trap of exaggerating our despicable nature and our degraded lives. True humility subdues our ambition and self-esteem without allowing us to become falsely modest.

Jesus Christ's life on earth is a supreme demonstration of humility. He was born in a stable surrounded by cattle; he grew up to be a carpenter in poverty in Nazareth; shortly before his crucifixion he was on his knees, a towel round his waist, washing the feet of his disciples, including those of Judas who he knew was to betray him. 'I am a servant among you,' he told them. This humble man was to become the founder of our Christian religion which has uplifted Christians throughout the world for two thousand years.

A living example of sublime humility is set by Mother Teresa. She and her sisters devote their lives to God's service and are known throughout the world. When asked about her work, Mother Teresa's reply is: 'I am just a little pencil in God's hands.' 'Doing something beautiful for God,' she says. Her example inspires rich and high caste Indian women to leave their wealthy surroundings and go down to her house in the slums of Calcutta. Here they humbly wash the feet and cut the toe nails of the sick and dying brought in from the streets. Yet these proud ladies would never dream of eating food contaminated by the mere shadow of one of these untouchables.

The following prayer was written by Mother Teresa:

'Lord, help us to see in your crucifixion and resurrection an example of how to endure and seemingly to die in the agony and conflict of daily life, so that we may live more fully and creatively. . . . Help us to accept the pains and conflicts that come to us each day as opportunities to grow as people and become more like you. Enable us to go through them patiently and bravely, trusting that you will support us. Make us realize that it is only by frequent deaths of ourselves and our self-centred desires that we can come to live more fully; for it is only by dying with you that we can rise with you.'

A Gift for God

For Mother Teresa this prayer has been answered by God. Let it be our prayer also.

~~~~~~

Nazareth

When I am tempted to repine
That such a humble lot is mine,
Within I hear a voice which saith;
'Mine were the streets of Nazareth.'

So mean, so common and confined,
And He – the Monarch of Mankind.
Yet patiently He travelleth
The narrow streets of Nazareth.

It may be I shall never rise
To place or fame beneath the skies,
But walk in lowly ways till death,
Narrow as streets of Nazareth.

Yet if thro' Honour's arch I tread,
And there forget to bend my head,
Oh, let me hear the Voice which saith,
'Mine were the streets of Nazareth.'

Author unknown. Quoted in *The Way of Love* by John Bagot Glubb

14 *Worship*

*Give unto the Lord the glory due unto his name: bring an
offering, and come unto his courts. O worship the Lord in the
beauty of holiness.*

Psalm 96.8, 9

~~~~~~

There exists in every human being, whether pagan or believer, a
need to worship a power greater than himself. Pagans worship idols
which the Bible tells us have eyes and ears and mouths but cannot
see, hear or speak. Believers worship their Creator. Christians bow
down and kneel before God the Father, Son, and Holy Spirit.

What do we mean by worship? Worship is lifting our heart to
God, using all our power to reach up to him. We all join together
in devoting ourselves to adoring God. Believing that he is the
sovereign good, we open our eyes to see his glory. To serve God we
must worship him.

Today our knowledge of science is undermining our belief in
God. When we no longer worship God, we worship ourselves. Like
pagans, we kneel down before idols. One of them at least, the
consensus of opinion, has a mind but cannot think. Other idols are
scientific inventions which enable us to reverse the laws of nature.
We pursue affluence, sensuality and leisure.

However much, like the psalmist, we love God's laws and hate
vain thoughts, in the world we are plagued with vain thoughts and
constantly tempted to disobey God's laws. The Church is here to
help us. We are inclined to think of a church or chapel as nothing
more than a building to which we go on Sundays to join our
brothers and sisters in the worship of God, to listen to sacred (or
sometimes, alas, profane) music, and hear some good advice. As
tourists we wander through cathedrals gazing in wonder at their
marvellous beauty; drenching the fragrance of incense with the
perfume of progress; buying a memento as we leave. Rarely do we
kneel down to pray.

But the church is more than a building. Despite differences of
creed and theology, the Church is one foundation. It is Christendom, in which Christ lives and reigns. The Church appoints leaders
– bishops, clergymen, and preachers. Their authority and discipline

28

should help us to love and obey God's laws and teach us to practise our religion and to serve God. Christ appoints his saints for every age. If we follow their example they will guide us through the dark world with its false idols, and open our eyes so that we are able to see the light of truth.

Then we shall truly learn to serve God with all our mind and all our heart and all our soul. Then we shall gratefully worship and adore him, not only with our lips but in our lives.

Let us, with a gladsome mind,
Praise the Lord, for he is kind:

For his mercies aye endure,
Ever faithful, ever sure.

Let us blaze his name abroad,
For of gods he is the God:

He, with all-commanding might,
Filled the new-made world with light:

All things living he doth feed,
His full hand supplies their need:

He his chosen race did bless
In the wasteful wilderness:

Let us then with gladsome mind
Praise the Lord, for he is kind.

John Milton

15   *Love*

Beloved, let us love one another: for love is of God; and every one that loveth is born of God, and knoweth God. He that loveth not knoweth not God; for God is love.

1 John 4.7, 8

Every human soul has experienced a longing for love. This longing is God's gift to man. It is his love in us. God is love and love is God. This awareness of God's love and the conviction that there exists another world, a world of the spirit where the soul dwells, remains a mystery. Reason cannot enlighten us. We must accept it on faith.

The first great commandment in the Bible is: 'Thou shalt love the Lord thy God with all thy heart, and with all thy soul, and with all thy mind.' The second is: 'Thou shalt love thy neighbour as thyself' (Matthew 22.37, 39). These two commandments are the first principles of our Christian religion.

In Dostoyevsky's novel *The Brothers Karamazov*, Father Zossima's discourse on love describes God's divine love:

> Brothers, be not afraid of men's sins. Love man even in his sin . . . Love all God's creation, the whole of it and every grain of sand. Love every leaf, every ray of God's light! Love the animals, love the plants, love everything. If you love everything, you will perceive the divine mystery in things. And once you have perceived it, you will begin to comprehend it ceaselessly more and more every day. And you will at last come to love the whole world with an abiding universal love . . . At some ideas you stand perplexed, especially at the sight of men's sins, asking yourself whether to combat it by force or by humble love. Always decide: 'I will combat it with humble love.' If you make up your mind about that once and for all, you may be able to conquer the whole world.

We cannot experience this divine love unless we keep our gaze fixed on the light of God's love that shines within our soul.

True love is always love for another. It makes a hard heart charitable and tolerant of sin. Christ who by his life and death showed his divine love for us, tolerated sinners. Knowing Judas would betray him, he knelt down and washed his feet, together

30

with those of the other disciples at the last supper. Nailed to the cross by his enemies, he called to God: 'Father forgive them for they know not what they do.' Let us follow his example and forgive our enemies and love sinners.

We cannot live without love. When we do not love another person we easily fall in love with ourselves. Mortal love is subject to human frailty. It soon becomes love of self, making us slaves to vanity, envy, and greed.

Michael Sellers wrote the following lines in *The Word of God and the Wisdom of Man*:

The beasts of the field say: 'Love made me.' The birds of the air say: 'Love made me.' The creatures that swim in the rivers and the sea say: 'Love made me.' Only man, his back turned to the sun, does not say 'Love made me.' But when he turns round in the light of Christ, then he too knows in his heart 'Love made me' and he cries out with every living creature, 'Love made me! My Father in heaven loves me.'

16 Saints

A little while, and ye shall not see me. And again, a little
while, and ye shall see me. . . . Then said some of his disciples
among themselves, what is this that he saith unto us, A little
while, and ye shall not see me: and again, a little while and ye
shall see me: and, because I go to the Father?

John 16.16–17

Throughout the years of Christendom men and women have been
born into the world with the spirit of truth in them. We call them
saints. G. K. Chesterton defined the transition of a good man into
a saint as 'a sort of revolution by which one for whom all things
illustrate and illumine God, becomes one for whom God illustrates
and illumines all things'.

We are familiar with the great saints of the Church through
whose lives and by whose writings God has illumined and illustrated
all things for us. They are messengers sent to remind us that Jesus
has fulfilled his promise that he would come again on earth to live
in us as he lived in the blessed Virgin Mary's womb two thousand
years ago.

St Augustine's *Confessions*, Thomas à Kempis's *Imitations of
Christ*, St Thomas Aquinas's *Summa Theologica*, St Teresa of Avila's
Life of Prayer, and St Teresa of Lisieux's *Life of a Soul* are all
classics which awaken the soul. These saints are God's advocates
who, inspired by the word of God, illumine our spiritual perception.

There are saints who illumine the word of God by their clowning.
St Francis wore his clothes inside out and walked on all fours to
demonstrate the follies of mankind. These 'fools for God' are like
the punk people of today and must beware of becoming the Devil's
advocates.

There are also many saints whom only God recognizes. We have
all met men and women who pour out a kind of balm which
comforts our soul.

All saints have the beauty and fragrance of holiness about them
and the scent of roses and violets and sweet-smelling flowers are
often associated with them. They bring the light of Christ into the
world – which is why artists always paint them with haloes.

Jean Pierre de Caussade describes how the sequel to the New

Testament is continually being written by saintly souls. Mother Teresa is one of them. She continues God's divine purpose in her life. She contradicts in word and deed every cherished fantasy and lie propagated by the media in this overwhelmingly materialistic age. And yet she is hailed by one and all as a saint. Neither media publicity nor world-wide praise have devalued the sublime truth of her words. So let us pray with her:

> Dearest Lord, may I see you today and every day in the person of your sick, and, whilst nursing them, minister unto you. Though you hide yourself behind the unattractive disguise of the irritable, the exacting, the unreasonable, may I still recognize you, and say: 'Jesus, my patient, how sweet it is to serve you.'
>
> *A Gift for God*

~~~~~~

If we study the lives of the saints we find that each saint says: 'Be ye followers of me as I am of Christ.'

From *The Notebooks of Father Bernard Vaughan*

How beautiful upon the mountains are the feet of him that bringeth good tidings, that publisheth peace.

Isaiah 52.7

17   *Images*

*The idols of the heathen are silver and gold, the work of men's
hands.*
*They have mouths, but they speak not; eyes have they, but they
see not;*
*They have ears, but they hear not; neither is there any breath in
their mouths.*
*They that make them are like unto them: so is everyone that
trustest in them.*

Psalm 135.15–18

Thus the Bible warns us of the danger of setting up idols and
worshipping images. History repeats itself. Today, our idols are
technology and computers. We sit at its feet and worship the 'box',
a contemporary 'burden of the valley of vision' (Isaiah 22.1) which
brings all the noise and tumult of the world into our living room.

We walk through the streets, earphones pouring into our ears
media messages of sex, violence and disaster – we are in a valley of
the shadow of death. Technology is replacing the human teacher,
and children learn to read, write and add by computer.

But television can only reflect an image of what is in front of the
camera, never the reality. Similarly, we can only reflect an image
of what we see with our eyes, not the reality. Only when we look
out *from* our mind *through* our eyes, and understand, can we see
what is real. William Blake understood this when he wrote:

> This Life's dim Windows of the Soul
> Distorts the Heavens from Pole to Pole
> And leads you to Believe a Lie
> When you see with, not thro' the eye.

'The Everlasting Gospel'

Let us beware of too much viewing and too much listening. We
are in danger of becoming a computerized collectivity with empty
souls – slaves of the media. The computer speaks to us in 'double-
speak', through robots who 'have minds but think not'. If we trust
them we shall indeed become like them. Theirs is the voice of the

consensus, the 'Big Brother' of George Orwell's horrific fantasy *1984*, telling us what we must think.

We can only stem this tide that threatens to drown us by seeing through our eyes into the light within us and looking for Jesus there. And if we look we shall find him.

The poet Cowper, who wrote the following verses was, like Blake, considered mad.

> *O! for a closer walk with God,*
> *A calm and heav'nly frame;*
> *A light to shine upon the road*
> *That leads me to the lamb!*
>
> *The dearest idol I have known,*
> *Whate'er that idol be;*
> *Help me to tear it from thy throne,*
> *And worship only thee.*
>
> *So shall my walk be close with God,*
> *Calm and serene my frame;*
> *So purer light shall mark the road*
> *That leads me to the lamb.*

18 *Money*

Godliness with contentment is great gain. For we brought nothing into this world, and it is certain we can carry nothing out. And having food and raiment, let us therewith be content. But they that will be rich fall into temptation and a snare, and into many foolish and hurtful lusts, which drown men in perdition. For the love of money is the root of all evil: which while some coveted after, they have erred from the faith, and pierced themselves through with many sorrows.

1 Timothy 6.6–10

Mammon, or Money, is the idol of an affluent society. 'Fiat Money' is the prayer of its citizens who worship in the supermarket according to the gospel of the advertiser's catalogue. The love of money tempts us to want more than we need for our daily bread. Judas loved money and so betrayed Jesus for thirty pieces of silver. Too late, he repented. Throwing the silver down, he went and hanged himself. Midas, King of Phrygia, loved money and so he prayed that all he touched might turn to gold. His prayer was answered but as the magic touch extended to food and drink he found it a doubtful blessing. For the love of money women are prepared to rent their womb for £13,000 a pregnancy. Yet the pursuit of wealth never brings us joy or contentment.

Civilizations in pursuit of wealth have always ended in corruption and ruin. What is happening in the West today is a repetition of history. Riches can only indulge the insatiable demands of our lust, vanity and pride for which enough is never enough.

For love of money, violence and depravity are shown on television screens at peak viewing hours, recorded on video tapes and reported in the press, demoralizing all who look and listen. Video tapes are available to children, who watch this demonic entertainment with the same spellbound fascination with which they used to listen to fairy tales about witches who arrived from their covens riding on broomsticks and turned their victim into a monster with horns and a tail. In these circumstances it is not surprising that law and order is breaking down. Murder, vandalism and depravity are threatening civilization as we have known it. We must beware that we, too, are not bewitched.

The love of money is like an evil spell which keeps us captive in the dark world of fantasy. We cannot love God and Mammon. Only by loving God are we released from our prison and free to live in the light of spiritual reality.

In the eighteenth century, the poet Oliver Goldsmith described the contentment of the man for whom enough was enough; who had not succumbed to what Professor R. H. Tawney some years ago called 'the unbridled indulgence of an acquisitive society' where wealth accumulates and men decay:

> A time there was, ere England's griefs began
> When every rood of ground maintain'd its man;
> For him light labour spread her wholesome store,
> Just gave what life requir'd, but gave no more:
> His best companions, innocence and health;
> And his best riches, ignorance of wealth.
>
> From 'The Deserted Village'

19 *Happiness*

Who so trustest in the Lord, happy is he.

Proverbs 16.20

The pursuit of happiness, according to the American Declaration of Independence, is a sacred and inalienable right. Happiness is sacred, but it is not a right or inalienable. Nor can it be subject to party politics or bought for money. It is something that all men long for. In his 'Essay on Man', Pope wrote:

> Oh Happiness! our being's end and aim!
> Good, pleasure, ease, content! whate'er thy name:
> That something still which prompts th' eternal sigh,
> For which we bear to live, or dare to die.

Yet if we pursue happiness we shall never find it. Very soon we destroy it, as savage beasts destroy their prey. For the pursuit of happiness soon turns into the pursuit of pleasure and leisure. But these are only phantoms of delight. Pursuing pleasure leads to an insatiable greed for whatever gratifies our senses and ends in debauchery. Pursuing leisure leads to boredom and finally to despair.

Samuel Johnson in the *History of Rasselas* describes the Happy Valley whose inhabitants are imprisoned in those phantoms: 'They wandered in gardens of fragrance and slept in the fortresses of security . . . Revelry and merriment was the business of every hour from the dawn of morning to the close of even.' Sitting down to eat and getting up to play was the business of every day, and everything was done to fill up the tedium of time. Only the hero, Rasselas, could find no happiness. 'I have seen,' he sighs, 'the sun rise and set for twenty months, an idle gazer on the light of heaven.' From that moment he 'bent his whole mind on the means of escaping from the valley of happiness', finding nothing but boredom imprisoned in the tedium of time.

Happiness on earth is never lasting. If not pursued, it comes and goes, like rays of sunshine breaking through the dark clouds on a rainy day, and then disappearing again, leaving behind a rainbow in the sky like a ray of hope. From time to time, during our pilgrimage on earth, God sends beams of happiness to assure us of his love. It is a sign of his grace.

Happiness is friendship and laughter; it is a loving companion; it is loving our neighbour; it is a lovely day; it is the beauty of the earth; it is the sweet content and peace which occasionally overwhelms us and which we cannot account for. But far surpassing all these and many more is the sublime happiness of finding God and loving him.

Happiness of heart can no more be attained without God than light and sunshine can be had without the sun. Happiness is heavenly born; its aroma is of heaven; it leads to heaven and its emblem is heaven.

On every side, in every part of the universe men and women are seeking happiness and cannot find it because they do not seek it from God.

From *The Notebooks of Father Bernard Vaughan*

20 *Work*

If any would not work, neither should he eat.

2 Thessalonians 12.2

In defiance of St Paul's warning, another somewhat disparaging phrase 'the work ethic' is often used by those in pursuit of the fantasy of leisure and pleasure. But in reality, every creature, including mankind, must work in order to live. Life without work is unbearable to man.

Tolstoy, in one of his wonderful parables, describes how, in Patagonia, God first creates men who have no need to work in order to provide themselves with shelter, clothing and food. Time passes and God looks down to see how they are faring. He finds that far from rejoicing in their lot, they are making life a curse instead of a blessing. So he decides to make it impossible for men to live without work, and turns Adam and Eve out of the Garden of Eden to build their houses, till their ground, tend their flocks and multiply. Then God says to himself, 'Certainly no man can reap and sow and spin and raise cattle alone. He will soon see that the more he works together with his fellow men the more they will produce and the more united they will become.' Time passes and once again God looks down on earth, only to see that men are even worse than before. They exploit each other and waste their time and energy quarrelling. So God decides to leave mankind alone. For some time they live as before without understanding how they can live and work together happily. At last one man discovers that the only way in which work can become a source of joy uniting all men together, is for them to be united in love.

At present the possibility looms large that very soon machines will be invented which will replace the work of men's hands and produce all we need, leaving us twenty-four hours a day for leisure and pleasure. This is an alarming prospect. We all know that the devil has work for idle hands to do. But fortunately for us all, so also has God. His work is plentiful and always available. We can seek out the sick and suffering who need comforting. We can bring hope to those in despair. We can devote our time and energy to helping those unable to help themselves. God is not mocked, for love is not subject to trade union rules. It is an impulse in each individual's soul, inspired by the love of God. A man does much if he does the work of God.

~~~~~~

Only The Master shall praise us, and only The Master shall
*   blame;*
And no one shall work for money, and no one shall work for
*   fame,*
But each for the joy of working, and each in his separate star,
Shall draw the Thing as he sees It, for the God of Things as
*   they Are!*

Rudyard Kipling, from 'When Earth's Last Picture'

21   The Way is the Way

Jesus said, 'I am the way, the truth and the life.'
'You have not chosen me, but I have chosen you, and ordained
you, that you should go and bring forth fruit.'
   John 14.6; 15.16

~~~~~~

During our pilgrimage on earth we are continually tempted by the love of wealth, power and vanity, to follow the way of the world. To our human eyes that way is alluring. It holds out the promise of rich rewards, of fame, success, and flattery. It offers a sunny and pleasant prospect of leisure and pleasure. Alas, this way does not fulfil our expectations! Fame, success and riches arouse envy, hatred and resentment. In his book, *An Unknown God*, Father Jonathan Robinson warns that although we must not hate the world we must not expect that it will bring us lasting happiness if we follow too much the devices and desires of our hearts. Whether we are followers of the way of the world or of the way of God, we are all put to the test and have to endure much tribulation and humiliation.

'In life there are two alternatives. Power and Love. No man can have both.' Those words were written by a Roman legionary on a stone tablet which was found in the Egyptian desert. It is for us to choose between the love of power, the way of the world, and the power of love, the way of God.

God sends trials to all of us to humble our pride. John Bunyan in *The Pilgrim's Progress*, describes how the pilgrims met with all manner of trials on their way to the celestial city. But Mr Great Heart was always by their side to help them out of their difficulties, as God will be by ours ready to help us on our way to him.

Each one of us must decide which way to take.

But while the day lasts, while the journey is still in progress, while we still have strength and health – before the shades lengthen and the busy world is hushed – while there is yet time let us turn to the Christ . . . who followed the same, often weary, road that is ours to follow. The Christ who in this dry and pathless land has promised us the living water welling up to eternal life.

   Father Jonathan Robinson, *An Unknown God*

If we choose the way of the world we shall find power. If we choose the way of God we shall find love. 'Some have wished that they might be troubled no more with either hills or mountains to go over. But the way is the way and there is an end' (from *Pilgrim's Progress*).

~~~~~~

He that is down, needs fear no fall,
He that is low, no pride:
He that is humble, ever shall
Have God to be his Guide.

I am content with what I have,
Little be it, or much:
And, Lord, contentment still I crave,
Because thou savest such,
Fullness to such a burden is
That go on Pilgrimage:
Here little, and hereafter Bliss,
Is best from Age to Age.

John Bunyan

22   The Cloud of Knowing

*Knowledge puffeth up. . . . If any man think that he knoweth
any thing, he knoweth nothing yet as he ought to know.*

1 Corinthians 8.1, 2

It used to be said that a little knowledge is a dangerous thing.
Today the same thing can be said of a lot of knowledge. In our
century, with the rapid advance of technology, men have discovered
how to fly to the moon, to walk in space, to make defence weapons
which will destroy the world with one big bang, to analyse sick
minds, to build machines to do a man's work. Despite this, what
we call our western civilization seems ever nearer to collapse. There
hasn't been a great rush to the moon. Astronauts haven't discovered
God in space. More food is being produced in the West than can
possibly be eaten there, but no one seems to know how to get food
to the starving populations in the third world. Psychiatric wards
are more crowded than ever. Unemployment is causing chaos.
Confusion and terror prevail.

Why, we ask ourselves? The reason is that knowing 'how' cannot
answer the question 'why?' 'Science sees everything from the
outside, even what is inside.' (Michael Sellers, *The Word of God
and the Wisdom of Man*.)

The vainglorious pretensions of science and technology have
made men proud and arrogant. They have knowledge but no
understanding. Knowing how is an escape from believing. It is a
challenge to faith. Knowing is not the truth. 'Only the truth shall
make us free.'

A fourteenth century monk told his disciple that God could
never be seen or known: 'The most godly knowing of God is that
which is known by unknowing.' A cloud of unknowing, he said,
hangs between man and God. In that cloud he must look for God.

Three centuries ago, Blaise Pascal, the brilliant mathematician
and scientist, who devoted his life to science, reached the same
conclusion. At the end of his life he admitted that all the discoveries
he had made amounted to nothing. Faith in God was the only
reality. More recently, a patient in a psychiatric hospital discovered
this too. 'Do you believe in God, Father?' he asked the visiting
priest.

44

'I do,' was the reply.

'Well, the psychiatrist in this place doesn't.' After a moment's reflection he added, tapping his forehead with his forefinger: 'He must be mad!'

We may be blinded by the dazzling light of knowledge shining on the natural phenomena of the world in which we live. Only the light of faith can shine through that cloud of unknowing, can open our eyes and bring us closer to God.

~~~~~~

Where shall wisdom be found? and where is the place of understanding? Man knoweth not the price thereof; neither is it found in the land of the living. The depth saith, It is not in me: and the sea saith, It is not with me. It cannot be gotten for gold, neither shall silver be weighed for the price thereof . . . for the price of wisdom is above rubies. . . . Whence then cometh wisdom and where is the place of understanding? Seeing it is hid from the eyes of the living. . . . God understandeth the way thereof. . . . And unto man he said, Behold, the fear of the Lord, that is wisdom; and to depart from evil is understanding.

Job 28.12–28

23   The Bible

*For the word of God is quick, and powerful, and sharper than
any twoedged sword, piercing even to the dividing asunder of
soul and spirit, and of the joints and marrow, and is a discerner
of the thoughts and intents of the heart.*

Hebrews 4.12

Those who are aware that there is something more to life than the
unreal fantasies of our human existence on earth, will look in vain
for truth in Darwin's Theory of Evolution, in philosophical
speculations about natural morality, in scientific propositions about
the universe, or in theological treatises on the meaning of conscience. All these will only plunge them into deeper confusion.
The dilemma still remains: how are we to discover what is real and
what is unreal?

Only the Bible can show us how we may live in the spirit, when
we are plagued by the dark fantasies of Power, Ambition, Pride,
Envy, Malice and Vanity. In the Ukraine, copies of the Bible
written out by hand were secretly circulated and read by believers.
For what other book would this labour have seemed worthwhile?
In *Up from the Rubble*, a book by a number of Russian dissidents,
the plight of believers deprived of their Bibles is poignantly
described:

> In the provinces, believers are reduced to blotting out the anti-
> religious patter in atheist pamphlets, leaving only the quotations
> from the Scriptures intact. I cannot forget the old man I saw on
> the steps of a Moscow church. 'Christian people,' he was saying,
> 'I'm from Kursk – everything we had has been burned. Couldn't
> anyone give me just one small book about God – please, in the
> name of Christ!'

No other book has been read by so many and for so long. The
authority of the Bible has been recognized for many centuries:

> What scholastics like Thomas Aquinas devoted their lives to
> studying, and a Blaise Pascal saw as one of the great realities in
> a world given over to fantasy; what a Michelangelo and a
> Leonardo da Vinci portrayed with such frenetic industry and

46

inspiration, and a William Blake, a Johann Sebastian Bach and a Feodor Dostoyevsky found a major source of illumination; what Tolstoy was ready, not just to accept as uniquely true, but as providing unique insights into the nature of man, his earthly existence and heavenly prospects, insights which he wove into the very texture of his thought and writing.

From a lecture delivered by Malcolm
to the Bible Society in Canberra in 1976

Today the Bible is no longer the dominating influence of our lives. It continues to be read as history but the mystical element is missing. Yet we cannot afford to ignore the testimony of so many great men of the past. If we are looking for help to guide us on our way through life, we must read, mark, learn and inwardly digest what is written in the Holy Scriptures. Here we shall discover God's truth, and Jesus who lives with us and in us. We shall open our eyes and confront the fantasy of man's wisdom with the reality of God's word.

For I am persuaded, that neither death, nor life, nor angels, nor principalities, nor powers, nor things present nor things to come, Nor height, nor depth, nor any other creature, shall be able to separate us from the love of God, which is in Christ Jesus our Lord.

Romans 8.38–39

24 Parables

*And the disciples came, and said unto him, Why speakest thou
unto them in parables? He answered and said unto them,
Because it is given unto you to know the mysteries of the
kingdom of heaven, but to them it is not given . . . Therefore
speak I to them in parables: because they seeing see not; and
hearing they hear not, neither do they understand.*

Matthew 13.10–11, 13

~~~~~~

The words of the New Testament have had more influence on the
western world and its peoples than any other words. It is the more
remarkable, therefore, to note that their essential truths are set
forth, not in the form of philosophical arguments but by means of
parables – simple stories that illustrate some moral or spiritual
point. For instance, the parable of the Good Samaritan, which
explores the question, 'Who is our neighbour?' or the parable of
the Prodigal Son which considers the question of family relation-
ships. Jesus, whose ministry is what the New Testament is about,
was fond of saying that children and simple folk would understand
what he was getting at better than highly educated intellectuals
and lawyers. The sophisticated Pharisees and Scribes, he knew,
would scorn his parables. How surprised they would have been to
know that for twenty centuries Christians everywhere, of all
degrees of education and of none, would cherish these parables,
deriving from them wisdom, virtue and entertainment.

The essential truths conveyed in the teaching of Jesus are
illustrated in nature's parables, of which there are many examples.

Perhaps the life of the caterpillar is one of the most striking. The
caterpillar (which represents the body) crawls over the earth
munching leaves, unable to look up into the sky where the butterfly
(the soul) flutters overhead. He weaves round himself a cocoon
(sin). After a while he emerges from his self-made prison – a
beautiful butterfly, off to heaven. It is a powerful image of the
incarnation: the birth, death and resurrection of Jesus which we
celebrate during Lent.

Writers have always drawn on nature's parables to present moral
truths about our human circumstances. In the tenth century BC the
sage Aesop wrote his fables or parables from nature. The Greeks

48

believed that they revealed the truth. With Christianity, a spiritual dimension was added. Today, when many people believe in the infallibility of facts, and moral laws are being debased, if not abandoned, those looking for truth will find it in parables whether they be nature's or Christ's.

~~~~~~

The Lion and the Rat

A rat popped out of his hole right between a lion's paws. The king of beasts spared the rat's life . . . It so happened that the lion was caught in a net from which his roars were powerless to free him. Sir Rat ran up, set to work with his teeth, and gnawed through the whole net.

'Patience and perseverance achieve more than violence and anger,' was the wise Aesop's sound conclusion.

25 *The Lord's Prayer*

But thou, when thou prayest, enter into thy closet, and when thou hast shut thy door, pray to thy Father which is in secret; and thy Father which seeth in secret shall reward thee openly.

Matthew 6.6

Not a day has passed since the beginning of Christianity when the Lord's Prayer had not been on the lips of Christians. It is an act of recognition, adoration, hope, petition, obedience and dependence.

How easy it is to pray only with our lips. Saint Teresa of Avila told her sisters that it was better not to pray at all than to pray only with our lips, without the attention of our mind.

Our Father which art in heaven, hallowed be thy name. Thy kingdom come. Thy will be done in earth, as it is in heaven. Give us this day our daily bread and forgive us our trespasses as we forgive them that trespass against us. And lead us not into temptation, but deliver us from evil: for thine is the kingdom, the power and the glory, for ever and ever. Amen.

As the familiar words fall from our lips we must understand them with our minds and feel them in our heart.

We direct our prayer to God through Jesus. We pray to our Father, unknown and unseen, whose existence is revealed in our human conscience and in our human love and in the beauty of the world around us. We praise his unknown name. We pray that his Kingdom, and not Satan's, will prevail. We pray that his will shall be done, not ours, on earth as it is in heaven. We pray for our daily sustenance; that our sins will be forgiven as we forgive those who sin against us. We pray for deliverance from the fantasies of our worldly condition. We acknowledge God's eternal power and glory.

In *Waiting on God*, Simone Weil presents a spiritual interpretation of the Lord's Prayer:

The six petitions correspond with each other in pairs. The bread which is transcendent is the same thing as the divine name. It is what brings about the contact of man with God. The kingdom of God is the same thing as his protection stretched over us against temptation; to protect is the function of royalty. Forgiv-

50

ing our debtors their debts is the same thing as the total acceptance of the will of God. The difference is that in the first three petitions the attention is fixed solely on God. In the three last, we turn our attention back to ourselves in order to compel ourselves to make these petitions a real and not an imaginary act.

No prayer can be compared to the Lord's Prayer. It includes everything we need to pray for or about. If we say it with our lips, understand it with our mind, and feel it in our heart, it will draw us closer to union with Jesus.

We must pray, pray, pray. If our prayer is deep, all the better. But should we encounter distraction, we still must pray. And whoever perseveres at it will obtain what he asks — like the man in the Gospel who had recourse to his friend for bread in the middle of the night.

James Alberione, *Thoughts*

26 Why Pray?

Prayer . . . God's breath in man returning to his birth,
The soul in paraphrase, heart in pilgrimage,
The Christian plummet sounding heaven and earth . . .
A kind of tune, which all things hear and fear;
Softnesse and peace, and joy, and love, and bliss . . .
Church-bells beyond the starres heard, the soul's blood,
The land of spices, something understood.

George Herbert, from 'Prayer'

Prayer is the heart of all religion. Prayer is the lifting up of our hearts to God. We are body and soul and spirit. The body is of the earth and returns to earth, but the soul lives in eternity, and in the soul breathes the spirit of God. We cannot exist spiritually unless we pray. It is through prayer only that we are able to escape from the turmoil of our bodily existence into the light of spiritual reality.

There are three degrees of prayer. Prayer of the lips, the mind and the heart.

Prayers of the lips are spoken prayers, in which we recite sacred words on our knees with bowed head. These require a great deal of patience and attention, for we easily repeat the words while our thoughts stray to quite other things, taking us back into the dark fantasies of the world.

Prayers of the mind are when, with our thoughts focused upon the written word, we pray consciously and silently.

Prayers of the heart are prayers which hitherto were explicit, but have now become feeling, and are offered from the depth of our being, silently. They cannot be comprehended for they transcend thought and go beyond the limit of consciousness, leading us to the light within. It is God's Spirit that prays in us.

How shall we pray?

With our lips – to be forgiven our sins, and to be determined to obey God's commandments and to resist evil.

With our mind – that the imagination of our heart may be acceptable in God's sight.

But with our heart, without words or thought, we reach up into a region closer to God. St Augustine in his *Confessions* describes his experience of this prayer. He and his mother, Monica, were looking

52

out of a window in Ostia, discoursing upon the mystery of the fountains of life. They had reached the point in their discourse where 'the very highest delight of the earthly senses were not worthy to be compared with the sweetness of that life,' when they 'soared higher yet' until they went beyond their minds into the region of feeling. Lingering there for a while, they then returned to earth, to 'vocal expression where words spoken have a beginning and an end', and to sigh after that 'one moment of understanding', that glimpse into eternity which has no beginning and cannot end.

God, humble my pride, extinguish the last stirrings of my Ego, obliterate whatever remains of worldly ambition and carnality, and, in these last days of a mortal existence, help me to serve only Thy purposes, to speak and write only Thy words, to think only Thy thoughts, to have no other prayer than: Thy will be done.

M.

27 Meditation

O how I love Thy law! it is my meditation all the day. . . .
Thy testimonies are my meditation.

Psalm 119.97, 99

Meditation is not a vocation exclusively practised by men and women who live a religious life in convents and monasteries. Nor is it prayer. It is a meeting in the heart of the mind and the soul. It deepens our understanding of our human condition. It opens our eyes on a wider view of what is real.

We can all meditate. A priest tells us: 'The only rule I would suggest to you would be to keep a certain time fenced off each day in which, alone with God, you brought your life and everything in it to him.' But how can we meditate when our time and attention are constantly being drawn to the business of life? Meditation takes place deep in the heart, unconsciously, without interfering with the preoccupation of our mind with the duties of our daily life, whatever they may be. When we consciously return to it, we are aware of ever fresh revelations about the mystery of things.

Meditation reveals the truth about many things which seem incompatible with the idea of a loving God when they are looked at in the light of worldly wisdom. It will help us to understand the necessity of suffering, disappointment and temptation. Once we begin to meditate it will become a habit. However, we must take special care that our meditations are acceptable in the sight of God. In the world we are tempted to meditate on many things that are not acceptable. We can fall for the temptation of self-righteousness, for thinking ourselves holier than our neighbour. We can become critical of others and complacent about ourselves. We must remain humble and meek.

When we meditate we are pursuing truth because we love truth and wish to understand it. St Thomas Aquinas defines meditation as the 'act of gazing at truth'. And the truth we are gazing at is God's truth, as far as it can be seen in this world.

If we set a certain time apart each day for meditation we may well begin by repeating the following prayer:

Gather unto thyself, dear Jesus, lover of my soul, all my senses, my understanding, my memory, heart and will: cleanse my soul from all evil and distracting thoughts: enlighten my mind, enkindle my heart, inflame my will, that during this meditation I may come to know thee more intimately, to love thee more ardently and to serve thee more faithfully and fervently. Amen.

The Notebooks of Father Bernard Vaughan

Meditation brings us as near to God as we can get on this earth. It is the spirit of truth which the wisdom of the world cannot perceive.

My words and thoughts do both express this notion,
That Life hath with the sun a double notion.
The first is straight, and our diurnal friend;
The other Hid, and doth obliquely bend.
Our life is wrapt in flesh and tends to earth:
The other winds toward Him, whose happie birth
Taught me to live here so, that still one eye
Should aim and shoot at that which is on high;
Quitting with daily labour all my pleasure,
To gain at harvest an eternal Treasure.

George Herbert, 'Our life is hid with Christ in God'

28 The Blessed Sacraments

And as they were eating, Jesus took bread, and blessed it, and brake it, and gave it to the disciples, and said, Take, eat; this is my body. And he took the cup, and gave thanks and gave it to them, saying, Drink ye all of it; for this is my blood of the new testament which is shed for many for the remission of sins.

Matthew 26.26–28

There is an idea that there is nothing sacred or mystical about the Blessed Sacrament, that it is merely taken in memory of a very holy man who lived a long time ago on earth, just as on Remembrance Day we celebrate the memory of some brave hero who gave his life for his country. This notion was launched some years ago by, among others, the then Bishop of Birmingham, Bishop Barnes, when he had the Bread and Wine analysed before and after consecration and announced that no physical change had taken place! From this 'proof' there arose the secular notion that there is no reason why any lay man or woman should not administer the Blessed Sacraments, as though they were a kind of religious 'fast food' served up on the highway to heaven.

It is easy to find historical evidence that the founder of Christianity lived and died on earth about two thousand years ago. But what is astonishing is that since his death not one week has passed when the religious service of a Christian Church, known variously as Holy Communion, the Eucharist or the Mass, has not been celebrated and the Blessed Sacrament not been administered to someone by someone, somewhere in the world. This is a unique fact in the history of mankind. It can only be interpreted as mystical evidence of the incarnation and the fact that when we eat the sacramental bread and drink the sacramental wine we are partaking of the body and blood of Jesus.

The business of the Church is worship and the teaching of Christians. The high point in Christian worship is the celebration of the Lord's Supper and the repetition of Christ's words to his disciples. This is the Blessed Sacrament. The soul requires nourishment as well as the body and when we eat the body and drink the blood of Jesus we are feeding our soul.

A priest who has given his life to the service of God, who is trained to teach his flock the practice of the Christian religion, alone has hands and lips clean enough to taste the bread and the wine, lips pure enough to repeat the words of Jesus and a soul holy enough to call on God to bless the Sacraments so that the bread and the wine may become the mystical body and blood of Jesus. We must respond with a humble and a contrite heart by confessing our sins and asking for forgiveness before we dare to eat or drink this blessed sacrament.

~~~~~~

Understanding and inquiry should follow faith, not precede and weaken it. In this holy and most excellent Sacrament, it is faith and love that are all-important, and they work in secret ways. God, who is eternal, infinite, supremely mighty, does great and unfathomable things in heaven and in earth, and there is no understanding his wonderful works. If the works of God could easily be grasped by human understanding they could not be called wonderful or too great for words.

Thomas à Kempis, *The Imitation of Christ*

29   The Ten Commandments

The first of all the commandments is, Hear, O Israel; The Lord our God is one Lord: And thou shalt love the Lord thy God with all thy soul, and with all thy mind, and with all thy strength: this is the first commandment. And the second is like, namely this, Thou shalt love thy neighbour as thyself. There is none other commandment greater than these.

Mark 12.29–31

The animal kingdom has its laws; mankind have theirs and God has his. Lawlessness destroys civilization. Nations whose people do not abide by the laws of the land are soon torn by strife and contention and brought to ruin.

We read in the Old Testament that the commandments were divinely revealed to Moses, engraved on two tablets of stone. When he brought them down from the mountain they were destroyed by the idolators. Later they were restored and placed in the Ark which the Israelites carried round with them in their wanderings. Except for forbidding men to work on the Sabbath and to worship images, these commandments roughly corresponded to the rules of life that are necessary to enable men to live peaceably together. They belong to the natural law which was recognized, even before they were revealed to Moses, as the common property of mankind. This requires us to honour our father and mother and not to kill, commit adultery, steal, bear false witness against our neighbour or envy anything that belongs to him.

When Jesus spoke to his disciples at the Last Supper he told them: 'A new commandment I give unto you, That ye love one another; as I have loved you, that ye also love one another. By this shall all men know that ye are my disciples, if you have love one to another.' (John 13.34–35). This addition to the commandments brings a divine element to the natural law, which is essential for the practice of the Christian religion. If we obey it we shall obey all the rest.

Saint Teresa of Avila in a letter to her nuns pointed out that discovering our love to our neighbour is the surest sign of discovering our love to God:

Be assured that the more you advance in the love of your neighbour, the more you advance in the love of God . . . But alas! How many worms lie gnawing at the roots of our love to our neighbour! Self-love, self-esteem, fault-finding, envy, anger, impatience, and scorn. I assure you I write this with great grief, seeing myself to be so miserable a sinner against all my neighbours.

Obedience to the law of the animal kingdom ensures the survival of the fittest; obedience to the natural law ensures the survival of civilized man. But God's law ensures the survival of the soul.

If we learn his commandments by heart and bear them in our mind they will help us to turn a blind eye on the evil temptations we encounter on our journey through life. They will help us to look ahead and see the lights of the City of God shining in the distance.

Fear God, and keep his commandments: for this is the whole duty of man. For God shall bring every work into judgment, with every secret thing, whether it be good, or whether it be evil.

Ecclesiastes 12.13–14

30 Sin

For the wages of sin is death; but the gift of God is eternal life through Jesus Christ our Lord.

Romans 6.23

Pagans and believers have always admitted the existence of evil as well as good. We all have a conscience and recognize, for instance, that love is good and murder is evil. Many people in this age of enlightenment cannot understand how an almighty and loving God allows the existence of evil and sin. Surely, goodness is all we need.

But our conscience tells us that there is something in human nature besides our body. We call it our soul. Our body is subject to the fantasies of our earthly existence. But our soul is subject to the reality of the life of the spirit.

Our bodies are tempted by fantasies of power, pride, lust and envy, which hide from our soul the spiritual reality which is the truth and brings us close to God. Temptations will assail us as long as we live on earth. We must never give in.

Having fasted for forty days and forty nights in the wilderness, Jesus felt hungry. Then the tempter came to him and suggested that if he was the son of God, he could turn the stones into bread. Jesus replied: 'Man shall not live by bread alone, but by every word that proceedeth out of the mouth of God.' (Matthew 4.4). Then he was taken to the top of a high tower in Jerusalem and tempted to throw himself down, for surely God would save him from being dashed to the ground. Jesus replied: 'Thou shalt not tempt the Lord thy God' (Matthew 4.7). Lastly he was taken to the top of a high mountain from which could be seen all the kingdoms of the world in all their glory. All would be his if he worshipped his tempter. Then Jesus replied: 'Get thee hence, Satan: for it is written, Thou shalt worship the Lord thy God, and him only shalt thou serve.' After this it is not surprising that the tempter left him alone. Let us follow Jesus's example.

Even today that last temptation appears in an advertisement. It shows a picture of an outstretched palm of an enormous hand on which rest a television set, a record player, a video tape machine, a cassette, a computer, a calculator, etc. Written beneath is 'All this will be yours at the tip of your fingers.' This is how advertising is being used; it is an instrument tempting us to worship technology. We must be like Jesus and resist to the end.

Jesus came to live as man on earth, to demonstrate by his incarnation his perfect love and truth and to show us that it is necessary to die in the flesh in order to live in the spirit. In other words, we need good to reveal to us what is evil and we need evil to reveal to us what is good. How can we know what good is if we have never heard of evil?

Let us leave the last word to Solzhenitsyn who made this discovery lying on rotting straw in the Gulag:

> It was only when I lay there on rotting prison straw that I sensed within myself the first stirring of good. Gradually it was disclosed to me that the line separating Good and Evil passes, not through States, not between classes, nor between political parties either – but right through every human heart – and through all human hearts . . . And that is why I turn back to the years of my imprisonment and say, sometimes to the astonishment of those about me: '*Bless you*, prison!'

For the flesh lusteth against the Spirit, and the Spirit against the flesh: and these are contrary the one to the other: so that ye cannot do the things that ye would.

Galatians 5.17–18

31   *The Devil*

Submit yourselves therefore to God. Resist the devil, and he will flee from you.

James 4.7

~~~~~~

What is the Devil? Who is he? From the Bible we learn that 'The great dragon was cast out [of heaven], that old serpent, called the Devil, and Satan, which deceiveth the whole world' (Revelation 12.9).

Believing souls with sceptical minds, who believe in God but cannot accept the Devil, may not be satisfied with this explanation. Reason has never been able to define good and evil or even separate them. Nevertheless there is as much evidence of the Devil in the world as there is of God. We have all been caught in his trap.

In our earthly circumstances there is a similar duality. We are aware of sorrow and joy, hate and love, darkness and light, evil and good. So it is with the Devil and God. Do away with the Devil and we do away with God. We are left with atheism and superstition. God uses the Devil for his own purpose. It is by the Devil's temptation to do evil that our eyes are opened and we discover what is good and learn that it is only in eternity that there can be joy without sorrow, love without hate, light without darkness and good without evil.

The cleverest thing the Devil did, said G. K. Chesterton many years ago, was to make us believe that he doesn't exist. This makes it easy for him to use our good intentions for his own wicked purposes. What more profitable for good intentions than the three offers the Devil made to Jesus in the wilderness? He offered him plenty, with which to feed the starving; he offered him the power to work miracles, and power to rule over the kingdoms of the earth, and so make the world a better place. Jesus rejected them all. He said to Pilate: 'My kingdom is not of this world.'

The Devil's kingdom is of this world. He is God's adversary. He succeeds in aping God's word so cunningly that it is hard not to be persuaded by him. His advocate is television. His message is self not love. His law – 'Thou shalt pursue wealth, leisure, lust and vanity' – abolishes God's Ten Commandments. 'Health, wealth and happiness' is the Devil's motto.

> Fall'n Cherub, to be weak is to be miserable,
> Doing or suffering; but of this be sure,
> To do ought good never will be our task,
> but ever to do ill our sole delight.
>
> 'Paradise Lost'

Thus John Milton rebukes the Devil.

Some may ask why we need to resist the Devil's enticing fantasies. The answer is because they create a society with a perverted sense of good, marked by strife.

What can we do to resist being deluded by them? We must remember God's Ten Commandments and pray continually to Jesus to grant us strength to resist the Devil's temptation.

> *Fight the good fight*
> *With all thy might,*
> *Christ is thy strength*
> *And Christ thy right*
> *Lay hold on life and it shall be*
> *Thy joy and crown eternally.*
>
> J. S. B. Monsell

32   Lent

And the devil said unto him, If thou be the Son of God,
command this stone that it be made bread. And Jesus answered
him, saying, It is written, That man shall not live by bread
alone, but by every word of God. And the devil, taking him up
into a high mountain, shewed unto him all the kingdoms of the
world in a moment of time. And the devil said unto him, All
this power will I give thee. . . . If thou therefore will worship
me, all this shall be thine. And Jesus answered and said unto
him, Get thee behind me, Satan: for it is written, Thou shalt
worship the Lord thy God, and him only shalt thou serve. And
he brought him to Jerusalem, and set him on a pinnacle of the
temple, and said unto him, If thou be the Son of God, cast
thyself down from hence. . . . And Jesus answering said unto
him, It is said, Thou shall not tempt the Lord thy God.

Luke 4.3–12

The Christian message of Lent, of sin and penance, suffering and
self-denial, is not acceptable to many people of progressive
persuasion. The progressive aim in life is self-fulfilment, and the
pursuit of pleasure. Sin is considered an invention of spoilsports
and penance the unnecessary self-inflicted indulgence of a prude.

Lent is a commemoration of Christ's temptations in the wilderness and of his crucifixion; and a celebration of his resurrection.
Today we have fallen for those temptations of the devil, those
fantasies of power, to no avail. We are able to make mountains of
'bread', but cannot feed the starving populations of the world. A
man can walk in space without fear of being dashed to pieces by
stones, yet we cannot walk on our roads without risk of being run
over. We have the power, with nuclear weapons, to rule over the
kingdoms of the earth, but they grow more unruly every day. This
is progress in evil.

But as Christians we believe that sin and penance, suffering and
self-denial, the circumstances of our mortal existence, will deepen
our faith and bring us in sight of heaven. This is something that
cannot be achieved by political slogans, social theories or revolutions. It can only be achieved by faith. Our observance of Lent is
an act of faith. We follow Jesus in the wilderness and learn from his

temptations the traps that are set for us by the Devil on our journey through life. These help us to understand the meaning of Christ's crucifixion and resurrection and apply it to our lives. George Herbert in his poem 'Lent' tells us:

> 'Tis true, we cannot reach Christ's fortieth day;
> Yet to go part of that religious way
> Is better than to rest.
> We cannot reach our Saviour's purity;
> Yet are we bid, Be holy ev'n as he.
> In both let's do our best.

Jesus dies on the cross

Jesus, help me to understand the utter profundity and the simplicity of the life you came on earth to teach us. A total self-giving and a total love. You came to show us that we too can share in that universal love that you have for all creation, the beasts, the flowers, the sky, the birds, the sea and every thing under the sea (Revelation 5). Grant I pray you that more and more I may learn to share that 'oneness' in you.

Forgive, we beg you, all the divisions of Christendom. The church still asunder, the quarrels and discord. May we be aware that all this is a very great sin.

> *Lord, forgive us*
> *Christ forgive us*
> *Lord forgive us.*

33   *Individual Love and Collective Concern*

Verily I say unto you, Except ye be converted, and become as little children, ye shall not enter the kingdom of heaven.

Matthew 18.3

~~~~~~

To be converted is to reject fantasy and perceive what is true. An illustration of what Jesus was saying was recently brought to my notice. Father Bidoni, an Italian priest who has founded and looks after homes for disabled children, brought three of these children to tea with us at our home in Sussex. Rosalind, my granddaughter, ten years old, gazed at them fascinated, but was somewhat alarmed at the strange noises and gestures they made. When the time came for them to leave, we all went out to the waiting car to wave farewell. I looked at Rosalind, and was surprised to see her troubled countenance transformed and radiant with love and joy as she went smiling up to one of the boys and kissed him. Whereupon he responded with a shout of merry laughter as though he had awakened from a sad dream.

The merry shout and laughter were a telling contradiction of the view held by those who, 'concerned' about suffering, believe it can be abolished, and that it is kinder to such children to kill them at birth, or, if possible, before, in order to spare them a suffering and useless existence. It was this consideration that inspired legalized abortion, and is responsible for an unborn child being murdered every three minutes; the same attitude lies behind mercy killing, and euthanasia for the aged and infirm. The reality of love accepts suffering, and heals and enriches; the fantasy of 'concern' rejects suffering, and commits murder.

Mother Teresa, when asked what she sees as the difference between what she does and what social workers do, replied: 'Social workers, very useful and humane in their purpose, do it for an idea; we do it for a person.' In the film, *Something Beautiful for God*, she is asked why she picks up the sick and dying off the streets of Calcutta and salvages newly-born babies from dustbins. She replies by exultantly holding up a tiny baby girl, and saying: 'See, there's life in her!' Love teaches us what is real, and brings us nearer to Jesus who commands us to love one another as he has loved us. He loves us through his suffering on the cross; in loving, there must be suffering. This is reality.

It is also fostering fantasy to teach the practice of sex to young children without reference to its purpose, which is procreation, or to its condition, which is lasting love. It threatens their chance of ever discovering the reality of true love, and opens the way to addiction to sexual depravity and carnality. Jesus said that when anyone thus destroys their innocence, 'It were better for him that a millstone were hanged about his neck, and that he were drowned in the depth of the sea' (Matthew 18.6).

Mother Teresa reminds us that love begins in the individual. 'Love lives in homes,' and where there is no love, 'in the home begins the disruption of peace in the world'.

34 Children

Jesus called a little child unto him, and set him in the midst of them, And said, Verily, I say unto you, except ye be converted, and become as little children, ye shall not enter into the kingdom of heaven. . . . And whoso shall receive one such little child in my name receiveth me. But whoso shall offend one of these little ones which believe in me, it were better for him that a millstone were hanged about his neck, and that he were drowned in the depth of the sea.

Matthew 18.2–3, 5–6

As we commemorate Jesus's trial and crucifixion, we seem to hear a sinister echo of the crowd crying out: 'Crucify him! Crucify him!' It is the cry of the abortionist demanding the murder of unborn children. 'Abortion is the sacrifice prosperous nations make to the god of prosperity, the god of materialism' (Michael Sellers, *The Word of God and the Wisdom of Man*).

In the Old Testament, Rachel, Jacob's wife, asked 'Give me children, or else I die!' Now we more often hear: 'Give me no children or else let me die!' Nevertheless, children continue to be born in the third world and in the West. Created in love by their parents, they bring love and joy into the world. Thus the love and light of Jesus is for ever being brought into the world by the young, as it returns to where it came from with the old. 'Children's children are the crown of old men' (Proverbs 17.6). And children love their father's father. They have just arrived from where Granddad is going. The young are not yet attached to the world of fantasy and the old have lost interest in it. This is what they have in common.

We need only compare the faces of those who prefer murder to celibacy or chastity with those of Mother Teresa's Sisters of Charity, to realize the truth that 'God maketh the barren woman to be a joyful mother of children' (Psalm 113.9). There is always laughter and joy and hope in the homes where abandoned children are brought in from the streets and cared for tenderly by the sisters. The tender love and care of the sisters brings the love of Jesus to these poor orphans.

Who can resist sharing the triumphant laughter of a baby

tottering on its own feet for the first time towards its mother's outstretched arms? What mother can look down on the face of her sleeping child without a pang of tenderness in her heart; or hear the merry shout of children playing without rejoicing. This infant joy is described by William Blake in his *Songs of Innocence*:

> 'I have no name:
> I am but two days old.'
> What shall I call thee?
> 'I happy am,
> Joy is my name.'
> Sweet joy befall thee!
>
> Pretty joy!
> Sweet joy but two days old,
> Sweet joy I call thee:
> Thou dost smile,
> I sing the while,
> Sweet joy befall thee!

Poetry is the language of the soul. Our youthful wonder when we first open our eyes on the world around is celebrated in the following verse:

> *How like an Angel came I down!*
> *How bright are all things here!*
> *When first among his Works I did appear*
> *O, how their Glory did me crown!*
> *The World resembled his Eternity,*
> *In which my Soul did walk;*
> *And evr'y thing that I did see*
> *Did with me talk.*

> Thomas Traherne, from 'Wonder'

35 Marriage

*A man . . . shall be joined unto his wife, and they two shall be
one flesh. This is a great mystery. . . . Nevertheless let every
one of you in particular so love his wife even as himself; and the
wife see that she reverence her husband.*

Ephesians 5.31–33

Science envisages the possibility of making children by taking an
egg from a female womb and fertilizing it with male sperm, then
placing it in an incubator for nine months to become a human
child; a citizen of a collective society ignorant of love. Such a
disastrous event would abolish the need for marriage. However, as
long as religion lasts in the world, the institution of marriage will
prevail in one form or another. For religion tells us that children
are 'begotten not made'.

In the animal kingdom the casual union of the sexes for the
preservation of the species is merely a matter of instinct. But with
humans it has the added dimension of love. It is nature's way of
propagating the human species and God's way of propagating
human love. We call it marriage.

Christian marriage brings with it three blessings: the short-lived
rapture of physical love, the joy of children and the comfort and
enduring grace of spiritual love. It also brings with it responsibilities
to the church and to the state. We undertake to abide by the law
and remain married unless there are specific grounds for divorce.
We honour the vows we made in church to remain married 'for
better or for worse until death do us part'.

Abortion, contraception and easy divorce have introduced a
serious threat to the institution of marriage. Men and women can
now engage in casual sexual unions, like the animals, without
risking the inconvenience of offspring. Divorce is no longer a
difficulty. The word chastity is out of circulation. Matrimony is no
longer holy.

It is inevitable that in the course of time trouble and strife
between man and wife should occur. This is for the most part due
to our human vanity and egotism; but these differences can be overcome and every reconciliation strengthens the bond of love.
Trouble and strife are not occasions for breaking a marriage.

70

Overcome, they are its sure foundations for out of it all will come
the realization that:

> Loves mysteries in soules doe grow,
> But yet the body is his booke.
>> John Donne, from 'The Extasie'

~~~~~~

Whom God has joined let no man put asunder.

36   *Motherhood*

And Mary said, My soul doth magnify the Lord, And my spirit
hath rejoiced in God my Saviour. For he hath regarded the low
estate of his handmaiden: for, behold, from henceforth all
generations shall call me blessed. For he that is mighty hath
done to me great things; and holy is his name.

The Magnificat, Luke 1.46–49

In the West this view of motherhood is not commonly held.
Motherhood is more often considered an inevitable inconvenience
attending the ravishing enjoyment of sexual relations between a
man and a woman. But it is an inconvenience which the medical
profession are only too willing to overcome with their expertise and
helpful advice. Contraception, abortion and sterilization are readily
available with the aid of a little pill and the surgeon's knife. The
law, enthusiastic for the preservation of the quality of life, is
prepared to sacrifice the sanctity of life and has lent a willing hand
by legalizing abortion. Since the Act was passed, over two million
unborn babies have been murdered. Skin food manufactured out
of their foetus has contributed to the preservation of the quality of
complexions. We do not have to look very far beyond the evil
fantasy of this wholesale destruction of life, to see and understand
the sanctity of motherhood.

When I was young, motherhood was eagerly looked forward to
by most women. Those of us who were deprived of motherhood
for one reason or another were sometimes compensated by God
who promised to make 'the barren woman the joyful mother of
children'. This promise has been fulfilled for Mother Teresa's
Sisters of Charity who devote a mother's tender love and care to
orphans and children who have been rejected by their own mothers.

Our baby leaping inside us; the triumphant shout as soon as it
is born; the little head sleeping on our bosom; the eager sucking at
our breast; the indignant yells and the gurgling laughter from the
cot; all these fill our hearts with unspeakable tenderness and love.
We rejoice that God is using our motherhood, as he used the Virgin
Mary's for the incarnation, whereby Jesus lives in the soul of every
mother's child.

Motherhood is watching over our children, sending them off to school in the morning, being at home when they get back, washing dirty faces, punishing disobedience, cooking spaghetti and jam tarts, reading aloud in the evenings and listening to prayers at bedtime. And when the time comes for them to venture out into the dangerous world, motherhood means following them with love and prayers.

Motherhood is the crowning glory of a woman's life to which no worldly success or achievement can be compared. It is a sacred gift from God. It is a privilege which we abuse at our peril.

<hr>

I pray you, Jesus, for all the mothers throughout the world – may they be like your mother, obedient to do your will, self-effacing, trusting in you, loving their children as she did, with unselfish, self-denying, understanding, enduring love. Grant to them a knowledge of their great vocation, and help them always to be worthy of their calling.

From *Love is the key*. A pilgrim's miscellany

37   The Family

'So let us pray, let us pray together. England especially has always been known as a family-loving country, a family-loving people: it has always been such a beautiful example of love and unity in the family. Protect that with your lives. Protect it through prayer. Prayer gives you a clean heart. The fruit of prayer is always deepening of faith, and the fruit of faith is love, and the fruit of love is service. So bring back prayer into your family life, for the family that prays together stays together, and if you stay together, you will love one another as God loves each one of you.'

Mother Teresa

Almost all creatures, human and animal, feed and care for their young until they are fully grown. The exceptions are authoritarian collectivities such as bees and ants.

The human family on earth represents Christ's family in heaven. It is a testimony to what the gospel tells us.

The family is one of the strongholds of society. Today it is being threatened on every hand by fantasies of affluence and the pursuit of happiness that all too soon becomes the pursuit of pleasure. Television pours fantasies into our living rooms which watching children imitate. Drugs, smoking and alcohol are easily available to them, preparing them to become citizens of a permissive society. How sad it is on a beautiful summer's day to see a group of children sitting with vacant faces in a darkened room, staring into the 'box' at scenes of violence and eroticism. The fantasy that we can preserve the quality of life by abortion and mercy killing, destroys the sanctity of life. Self-fulfilment, in reality self-indulgence, prompts many women to look upon motherhood and home-making as uncreative, tedious and unfulfilling. They hand their children over to social workers to be cared for like orphans where no love is to be found. Easy divorce and the three-year marriage favoured by some clergy spell ruin to holy matrimony as laid down in the Book of Common Prayer. Chastity is no longer respected, and more marriages end in divorce than ever before.

All these are enemies of the family. What can be done to save it? Most important is that parents should be prepared to raise their family together, teaching them discipline and love. Marriage must be for life. Thus we shall make home a place of love and understanding and support; children will learn from the unselfish love and devotion of their parents to love for themselves, and to understand what God's love means, thereby transforming the fantasy of the pursuit of happiness into the reality of love.

Finally, brethren, whatsoever things are true, whatsoever things are honest, whatsoever things are just, whatsoever things are pure, whatsoever things are lovely, whatsoever things are of good report: if there be any virtue, and if there be any praise, think on these things.

Philippians 4.8

38 Suffering

In the world ye shall have tribulation: but be of good cheer; I have overcome the world.

John 16.33

~~~~~~

Suffering is part of life. We can share it and relieve it but we can never escape it. The mystery of why God allows us to suffer is rooted in redemption, in Jesus' suffering for us on the cross. His death and resurrection assure us of God's love and bring us hope in the world to come. It is a mystery only revealed to us in so far as we have faith. It is the evidence of things unseen.

Simone Weil, the French-Jewish mystic, explains this very clearly.

> It is in affliction itself that the splendour of God's mercy shines; from its very depths, in the heart of its inconsolable bitterness. If, still persevering in our love, we get to the point where the soul cannot keep back the cry: 'My God, why hast thou forsaken me?' If we remain at this point without ceasing to love, we end by touching something which is not affliction, which is not joy; something which is the central essence, necessary and pure; not of the senses, common to joy and sorrow, something which is the very love of God.

Suffering teaches us endurance, and by endurance, Jesus tells us we shall gain our lives.

> Suffering is the great teacher; the consecrated suffering of one soul teaches another. I think we have got all our values wrong; and suffering is the crown of life. Suffering and expansion, what a rich combination! . . . All deepened life is deepened suffering, deepened dreariness, deepened joy. Suffering and joy. The final note of religion is joy.
>
> Baron Von Hugel

Lourdes is a witness to this marriage of suffering and joy. Mother Teresa shows us that suffering can become a means to even greater love and generosity. It can be overcome and turned to joy.

Every time a child is born a mother suffers the pains of labour.

76

Joy comes when her baby is born. Alexander Solzhenitsyn, looking back on his imprisonment in a Soviet labour camp, declared that it was there, in all its horror, that he found his soul.

We must thank God for our suffering. For us, too, it can turn to joy. To discover joy and peace through our suffering we must surrender ourselves to the will of God. We must never be discouraged by grief or pain.

Edith Barfoot spent seventy years suffering.* Rheumatoid arthritis deprived her of motion, eyesight and hearing and yet to the end of her life there was about her a radiance and joy. She met all the difficulties imposed on her physical condition with cheerful determination and never lost heart. She gradually withdrew from the physical world to live more intensely in the world of the spirit where she found a vocation for suffering which she used to help, comfort and strengthen other suffering souls for the love of God.

Let us make use of our frailty, hardships, these cares, this need for food and clothing and possessions, these failures, suspicion of others, these doubts and anxieties, these perplexities, and find our joy in God who, through them, gives himself wholly to us to be our only blessing.

Jean Pierre de Caussade, *The Sacrament of the Present Moment*

Man was made for joy and woe;
And when this we rightly know
Thro' the World we safely go.
Joy and woe are woven fine,
A Clothing for the Soul divine;
Under every grief and pine
Runs a joy with silken twine.

William Blake, from
'Auguries of Innocence'

* *The Joyful Vocation to Suffering*, published by Basil Blackwell, 1977.

39   Old Age

I have been young, and now am old; yet have I not seen the
righteous forsaken, nor his seed begging bread.

Psalm 37.25

Old age is generally contemplated with dread and pity and some
are even reluctant to admit its inevitability. Such terms as
'geriatric', 'cabbage', 'second childhood', used to describe people
who are growing old, scarcely convey the respect and veneration
with which the aged used to be held when society was founded on
a belief in a Creator. Belief in the theory of evolution encourages
an attitude which is concerned only to maintain a high quality of
life, and is therefore inclined to discard specimens not coming up
to the required standard.

When there is no future before us we can only look back on our
past, for it is by so doing that we can understand the reason for all
that has happened to us. Thus moment by moment, day by day,
year by year, we learn from the experience of living. So we grow up
and so grow old.

There will be much cause for remorse and repentance, for which
we must pray to be forgiven: the irreparable wrongs we have done
to others, our absurd pride and vanity, our pitiful efforts to
overcome our sins and all the grief and suffering and failure of life
on earth. There will be happy memories, too, giving cause for
rejoicing and gratitude: the wonder of creation, the beauty of
goodness, the blessing of human love. And so, as we turn over the
pages of our book of life, many of them smudged and stained, we
shall see that it was not its trivial triumphs, nor even its fleeting
happiness, but the mistakes, the suffering, the affliction that have
been the means whereby our soul has been enlightened and has
come into contact with reality and even been afforded a glimpse
now and again of heaven.

When we have reached the age of retirement let us humbly
abdicate our role as active citizens in favour of a younger generation.
No longer preoccupied with affairs of the world, released from the
burden of ambition, life's fever abating, we are now free to devote
every minute of the time left us on earth to the things of the spirit.
Even our failing faculties of sight, hearing, memory, are no longer

a catastrophe but blessings. As we die in the flesh and live more and more in the spirit we learn to grow old with dignity. We can spend our time helping our neighbour, waiting on God, making as few demands on others as possible, not resenting our ebbing vitality, gratefully accepting the help we receive from others.

There are many delightful aspects of growing old. One is the unique bond we have with the very young. We seem to talk the same language. Perhaps this is because we have ceased to take an interest in world affairs while they have yet to begin. Seeing the world through dimming eyes we see ever more clearly the ravishing beauty of God's creation. Then, when we come to our final decrepitude, if we are not victims of euthanasia and are allowed to die a natural death, let us leave our body with relief to decay and corruption on earth, and may our soul pass with hope through the door that leads into eternity.

My retrospect of life recalls to my view many opportunities of good neglected, much time squandered up on trifles, and more lost in idleness and vacancy. I leave many great designs unattempted, and many great attempts unfinished. My mind is burdened with no heavy crime, and therefore I compose myself to tranquillity; endeavour to abstract my thoughts from hopes and cares, which, though reason knows them to be vain, still try to keep their old possession of the heart; expect, with serene humility, that hour which cannot long delay: and have hope to possess in a better state, that happiness which here I could not find, and that virtue which here I have not attained.

Dr Johnson, *The History of Rasselas*

40   *Death and Resurrection*

*So when this corruptible shall have put on incorruption, and this
mortal shall have put on immortality, then shall be brought to
pass the saying that is written, Death is swallowed up in
victory. O death where is thy sting? O grave, where is thy
victory?*

I Corinthians 15.54, 55

The death and resurrection of Christ is a vital fact in Christian
faith. It has been commemorated each Easter for two thousand
years.

Without faith we look forward to death with fear and apprehen-
sion. Did not Christ, in his manhood, falter momentarily, crying
out with a loud voice, 'My God, why has thou forsaken me?'

Geneticists juggling with genes, transplant surgery, and advances
in medicine, open up the prospect of prolonging life indefinitely.
But few of us look forward with enthusiasm to everlasting life on
earth.

In *Gulliver's Travels*, Jonathan Swift describes the immortal
Struldbugs, bored, dejected and despairing, watching funerals go
by, envious of the dead, longing to die themselves.

But if we have faith, death is no longer to be dreaded. Pastor
Dietrich Bonhoeffer, condemned to death by the Nazis, held a
small service while waiting to be taken away and executed. Payne
Best recalls:

He reached all our hearts, by finding just the right words to
express the spirit of our imprisonment. The service had scarcely
ended when the door was flung open and two men stood in the
doorway. 'Prisoner Bonhoeffer, take your things and come with
us.' As he gathered up his belongings, the last words he spoke
were, 'For me this is the end but also a beginning. I believe in
our universal brotherhood . . . and that victory is certain.'

A beautiful description of death in John Bunyan's *Pilgrim's
Progress* recalls the pilgrims reaching the end of their journey to the
Celestial City. They have fought with Giant Despair, been
imprisoned in Doubting Castle, escaped from Vanity Fair, and
battled many times with the adversary on their way.

There came a post . . . and his business was with Mr Ready-to-Halt. So he enquired him out, and said to him, 'I am come to thee in the Name of him whom thou hast loved and followed, tho' upon crutches. And my message is to tell thee, that he expects thee at his table to sup with him in his kingdom the next day after Easter. Wherefore prepare thy self for this journey.'

Then he also gave him a token that he was a true messenger, saying, 'I have broken thy golden bowl, and loosed thy silver cord.'

After this Mr. Ready-to-Halt called for his fellow pilgrims, and told them, saying, 'I am sent for, and God shall surely visit you also . . . And because he had nothing to bequeath to them that should survive him, but his crutches, and his good wishes, therefore thus he said: 'These crutches, I bequeath to my son that shall tread in my steps with an hundred warm wishes that he may prove better than I have done.'

When he came at the brink of the river . . . the last words he was heard to say, were: 'Welcome Life'. So he went his way.

Many years ago, I myself lay in hospital hovering between life and death. I seemed to look down on my lifeless body. I was aware of my beloved husband lying by my side, his blood dripping into my veins and my sweet children sad and silent round my bed. My heart was overwhelmed with tender love for them, and the 'peace that passeth understanding' filled my soul. Eternity did not open its door. Returning to my body, I experienced a pang of regret. This vivid memory has never left me.

And so on our journey through life we must not allow ourselves to become engrossed in the triviality of our earthly surroundings. If we continually strive to resist the temptations of lust, pride, anger and envy, when we reach the end we shall have learnt to live in the spirit and discovered everlasting truth. We shall meet death with hope, crying out like Bunyan's pilgrim, 'Welcome Life'.

Death be not proud, though some have called thee
Mighty and dreadful, for, thou art not so,
For, those, whom thou think'st, thou dost overthrow,
Die not, poor death, nor yet canst thou kill me. . . .
And poppy, or charms can make us sleep as well,
And better than thy stroke. Why swell'st thou then?
One short sleep past, we wake eternally,
And death shall be no more; death, thou shalt die.

John Donne, from 'Holy Sonnets'

*Bring us, O Lord, at our last awakening into the house and gate
of heaven, to enter into that gate and dwell in that house, where
there shall be no darkness nor dazzling but one equal light, no
noise nor silence but one equal music, no fears nor hopes but one
equal possession, no ends nor beginnings, but one equal eternity,
in the habitations of thy majesty and thy glory, world without
end.*

John Donne